I

This encyclopedia on demons is positioned within an academic framework, grounded in rigorous historical, cultural, and scholarly research. Its primary purpose is to offer an objective and factual compilation of information about demons, meticulously addressing mythologies, cultural beliefs, and historical representations in a precise and well-documented manner. Each entry aims to provide verifiable and contextualized data, ensuring an informative and educational approach for those interested in understanding the richness and diversity of demonic conceptions across various cultures and historical periods.

The Luciferian Lexicon

Editor-Illustrator: Ricardo Gallego

# THE LUCIFERIAN LEXICON A DEMONIC DICTIONARY

To all the intrepid explorers of the shadows and guardians of ancient darkness, this demonic encyclopedia stands as a tribute to your fascination with the enigmatic. May these pages serve as a portal to the mysteries that lie beyond the light, and may those who delve into its depths find both knowledge and delight in the dark dance of demons. To the lovers of shadows, whose hearts beat to the rhythm of the unknown, I dedicate this work with gratitude and admiration.

RICARDO GALLEGO

INITIATION

Knock, knock... Do you hear that mysterious tapping at the door? You peek, but no one is there. You wonder if your mind is playing tricks on you, if perhaps you imagined it. But without realizing it, you are opening the door to malevolent and shadowy forces, energies we do not understand, but know are there. We all have felt our skin prickle at some point or experienced sudden moments of sadness, anger, and desolation. Haven't you asked yourself that question? They are there, lurking in the shadows, invisible yet always present. Have you ever felt like you are being watched?

Even though there is much we do not understand about life, one thing is undeniable: demons have been silent companions on our journey through the centuries. They are elusive entities, lurking at the edges of our comprehension, immersed in the darkest mysteries. Through this cursed book, I will recount my own pilgrimage through the unknown, my search for answers in the world of the occult and the sinister.

In these pages, I will unveil the secrets, the names, and the stories of these infernal beings that have haunted humanity's nightmares. From the abysses of mythology to the darkest corners of popular belief, we will venture into a territory where the inexplicable mingles with the unnameable.

THE DARK ROADS

Since childhood, my life has been plagued by mysterious experiences and unsettling encounters that led me down the dark path of the paranormal world. I always knew something extraordinary was destined to happen. Before falling asleep, I would hear a strange sound, like the bounce of a basketball in an empty room. It was the prelude to nights filled with nightmares and visitors from another realm.

One of my most impactful experiences involved sleep paralysis. On one particular night, I found myself unable to move or scream as I watched a shadow move unnaturally, dark whispers filling the air. It was a terrifying sensation, as if the very abyss had opened before me.

My obsession with the paranormal deepened as I grew older. Strange noises in the dead of night and fleeting shadows at the corners of my eyes became a constant in my life. At times, vivid dreams blended with reality, making it difficult to discern between the two. Nightmares became a constant companion.

As I delved into my career as a writer, I began to investigate and document cases of demonic possession, cursed places, and paranormal phenomena. I had to experience it with all my senses. Each encounter left me with more questions than answers, fueling my insatiable passion for the inexplicable.

Here I stand, ready to explore the world of demons and the paranormal once more, determined to unveil the darkest secrets lurking in the shadows and share these unsettling stories with all who are willing to join me in the quest for the supernatural. Thanks to modern times, I have dared to recount my experiences and capture them with a precision that I could only dream of before. Now, with the ability to document and share these encounters accurately, I am more prepared than ever to embark on this mysterious journey.

The belief in demons has roots in antiquity and can be found in many different cultures and religions. In ancient Mesopotamia, for example, there were tales of a being called Arima, who was considered the prince of darkness. In the Canaanite world, to which the Hebrews belonged, there was a catalog of exorcisms and spells against malevolent demons.

In the Hebrew Bible, although the Israelite worship did not officially prescribe any means to defend against demons, several malevolent beings or spirits are mentioned. In Spiritist Doctrine, there are no angels and demons as such, but rather Spirits with moral characteristics that align with the descriptions of these creatures. In other words, there are beings who have advanced on their evolutionary journey and possess the virtues of "angels," as well as beings at lower levels of consciousness, resembling "demons."

The word "demonology" comes from the Greek "daimon," meaning "genius" or "demon," and "logía," which translates to "science." Throughout history, demonology has studied these beings from various perspectives and cultural contexts.

In short, belief in demons has developed over thousands of years as cultures, religions, and explanations for the unexplainable have evolved.

Demons have been used to personify evil and the unknown, and have played a prominent role in mythology and human psychology throughout history.

Beliefs in malevolent and demonic beings can be traced across multiple cultures and religions throughout history. Here is a general overview of some of the origins of these beliefs:

Ancient Mythology: In many ancient cultures, such as the Sumerian, Babylonian, Egyptian, and Greek, there were gods and entities believed to be responsible for both blessings and curses. Some of these deities or beings were perceived as malevolent or mischievous, and over time, their stories became part of demonic traditions.

Abrahamic Religions: The Abrahamic religions, including Judaism, Christianity, and Islam, have significantly influenced the concept of demons. In the Old Testament of the Bible, there are references to evil beings who oppose God. The fall of Lucifer and his transformation into Satan is an iconic example of this narrative.

Religious Syncretism: As cultures mixed and religions intersected, beliefs about demons also evolved. In many traditions, demons merged with local deities or supernatural beings.

Explanations for Evil and Disease: Throughout history, demons have been used to explain human suffering, such as illness, madness, or misfortune. This idea of malevolent beings inflicting suffering has persisted through the ages.

Unexplained phenomena: Unexplained or unusual phenomena were often attributed to the intervention of demonic beings. This includes everything from extreme weather events to incomprehensible human behavior.

HELL

The term "Hell" originates from the Latin "infernus" or "inferus," meaning "below," "lower place," or "underground." It is related to the Hebrew word "Sheol" and the Greek "Hades." According to many religions, Hell is the place or state where, after death, the souls of sinners are eternally tortured. It is equivalent to Gehenna in Judaism, Tartarus in Greek mythology, Helheim in Norse mythology, and the Underworld in other religions.

In Catholic theology, Hell is one of the four last things. The Catechism of the Catholic Church affirms its existence and eternity. The souls of those who die in a state of mortal sin descend to Hell immediately after death to suffer the pains or "eternal fire." The principal punishment is "eternal separation from God."

Hell has also been depicted in literature, such as in the famous work "The Divine Comedy" by the Florentine poet Dante Alighieri. In this work, Hell is described as a place of eternal punishment, where sinners suffer torments corresponding to the sins they committed in life.

Beyond these descriptions, Hell is a complex and multifaceted concept that varies greatly among different cultures and religious traditions. Some view it as a physical place of torment, while others interpret it as a state of separation from the divine. However, all these interpretations share a common characteristic: Hell is a place or state of extreme suffering, a dreaded destination for all who believe in its existence.

The concept of hell, the place of punishment for evil souls, has deep roots dating back to ancient civilizations. In Sumerian mythology, there was already talk of an underworld ruled by the goddess Ereshkigal, a shadowy realm to which souls descended after death. However, it was in Greek mythology that the concept of an underworld as a place of punishment and torment was consolidated. The Greeks believed in Tartarus, an abyss in the depths of the Earth where titans and other evil beings were thrown to suffer eternally.

This grim concept was inherited by the Romans, who adapted it into their own mythology, creating the concept of "Hell" as we know it today. In Roman mythology, Hell was ruled by Pluto, and the souls of the wicked suffered eternal punishments in his realm.

However, it was with the spread of Christianity that the concept of hell acquired even greater importance. The Christian Bible, particularly the New Testament, speaks of a place of eternal torment where sinners are condemned to suffer. Satan, a fallen heavenly figure, became the ruler of this dark place.

Throughout the Middle Ages, the idea of hell took root in European culture, and became a powerful tool in the hands of the Church to influence people's beliefs and behavior. The depiction of hell in art and literature became a visual manifestation of punishment and warning against sin.

The perception of hell has evolved and been interpreted in various ways by different cultures and religions. Whether as a realm of punishment or a metaphor for human suffering, hell remains an intriguing and mysterious concept that has endured through the centuries, influencing human spirituality, culture, and psychology. Who can claim to know its darkest secrets?

The concept of "hell" varies among different religions, mythologies, and belief systems, with a wide array of interpretations and representations of what hell might be. Here are some of the most well-known conceptions of hell:

Christian Hell: In Christian tradition, there is considered to be a single hell, often described as a place of eternal punishment for condemned souls. Hell is commonly associated with Satan and his demons and is viewed as the antithesis of heaven, a place of torment and separation from God.

Islamic Hell: In Islam, there is a belief in a hell called "Jahannam." It is a place of punishment for sinners and is described in the Quran as a realm of blazing fire and eternal suffering.

Buddhist Hell: In some interpretations of Buddhism, there is mention of "Naraka," a type of hell where souls suffer as a consequence of their bad deeds. There are multiple levels of Naraka, each with a different degree of suffering.

Hindu Hell: In Hindu mythology, there is a belief in "Naraka," a realm of suffering and punishment for wicked souls. This concept is also intertwined with the ideas of reincarnation and karma.

Other Traditions: Various other religions and cultures have their own conceptions of hell. For example, in Greek mythology, there is Tartarus, a place of punishment for Titans and other malevolent entities. In Norse mythology, Hel is mentioned as a realm of the dead.

A theory that seeks scientific explanations beyond the spiritual might suggest that the notion of hell is the result of a complex interaction between human perception and quantum physics. According to this theory, hell, as described in different traditions, could exist in another dimension that coexists with our own.

Quantum physics has theorized the existence of multiple parallel universes, each with its own laws and realities. The "dimensions" theory suggests that some people might be more sensitive than others to the "boundaries" between these universes and dimensions. These sensitive individuals could experience visions, nightmares, and paranormal phenomena that seem to connect with a world beyond our understanding.

In ancient times, when people witnessed these inexplicable manifestations, they might have interpreted these experiences as encounters with demonic beings, and exorcisms could have been attempts to free individuals from these misunderstood influences.

Furthermore, in this theory, the interaction between the dimensions could have had an impact on people's mental health. Those who were particularly sensitive to these "borders" between dimensions might have experienced mental problems due to the stress of living in two different realities.

This theory provides a potential scientific explanation for experiences that have traditionally been interpreted as demonic or hell-related. However, it is important to note that this is just a theory and that the existence of multiple dimensions and parallel universes is a concept still under discussion in the scientific community. Spiritual and religious beliefs also play an important role in how people interpret these experiences.

Hell is more than fire and brimstone. It is a reflection of our deepest fears and our deepest insecurities. It is a reminder of the eternal consequences of evil and a call to live our lives with righteousness and compassion.

PURGATORY

BETWEEN LIFE AND ETERNITY

The concept of purgatory has been an integral part of religious and spiritual beliefs in various cultures and religions throughout history. Although representations vary, it is generally described as an intermediate state or place between earthly life and eternity, intended to purify souls before reaching their final destination.

In Catholic Tradition: Purgatory is a key component of Catholic theology. It is considered a temporary state of purification for souls who have died in grace but who still must atone for their venial sins or resolve unfinished business before entering the divine presence. It is believed that the prayers and pious actions of the living can help speed up this process.

Perspectives in Other Religions: While the term "purgatory" is specific to Catholic theology, other religions have similar concepts. In some non-Catholic Christian traditions, such as Orthodox Christianity, the idea of a purification process after death is also present. Additionally, certain branches of Hinduism and Buddhism believe in cycles of reincarnation and the need to purify karma before reaching a state of liberation or nirvana.

Paranormal Experiences and Accounts: Paranormal experiences related to purgatory are difficult to verify, but throughout history, there have been numerous accounts of individuals claiming to have had visions or encounters with souls undergoing purification. These stories are often shrouded in mystery and carry a deep spiritual element.

Artistic Manifestations: Purgatory has inspired numerous literary, artistic, and cinematic works. From Dante Alighieri's Divine Comedy to contemporary films exploring themes of the afterlife, purgatory remains a fascinating subject that captures the imagination of creators and audiences alike.

In summary, purgatory presents itself as a mysterious bridge between life and eternity, weaving a tapestry of beliefs, traditions, and paranormal experiences. Its representation varies, but its essence lies in the pursuit of purification and reconciliation before taking the final step into the unknown.

SATAN

Satan, also known as Lucifer, was an angel of great piety and beauty. His name, meaning "Shining One" or "Bearer of Light," reflected his celestial status. However, Lucifer rebelled against God and was cast out of heaven. His name changed to Satan, meaning "adversary," "opponent," or "accuser." Yet Lucifer was not the only one to rebel. According to Christianity, other angels also disobeyed or rebelled against God's commands and were expelled from heaven. These fallen angels include Mephistopheles, Semyazza, and Azazel.

The Book of Enoch, an ancient manuscript written between the 4th and 1st centuries BCE, provides the most comprehensive source on the fallen angels. According to this text, the fallen angels were called Watchers or Grigori, celestial beings whom God sent to Earth to watch over and protect humanity during its early stages. In the Bible, the Book of Revelation describes a war in heaven between angels led by the archangel Michael against those led by "the dragon," identified as the devil or Satan. The rebellious angels were defeated and cast down to earth. Since his fall, Satan has become the ruler of hell and the chief adversary to the Kingdom of God. He is depicted as the serpent who deceives humans, urging them not to follow the Creator's precepts.

The story of Satan and the fallen angels has become an iconic tale reflecting the eternal struggle between good and evil. Satan, once a beautiful star of heaven, fell from grace due to his ambition and rebellion. Since then, he has been associated with sin, temptation, and evil in Christian theology and demonology.

The fallen angels narrative also raises profound questions about the nature of rebellion, free will, and redemption. Can a celestial being fall so low? Is there hope for redemption even for fallen angels? These questions continue to intrigue those who explore the mysterious and the paranormal.

THE GARDEN OF EDEN

In the famous tale of the Garden of Eden, it is recounted that Satan took the form of a serpent to tempt Eve and Adam. However, it is important to note that there is no explicit mention of the devil or Satan in the Book of Genesis. It was only later that Christians interpreted the serpent as an incarnation of Satan.

The serpent, with its cunning and deceit, convinced Eve to eat the forbidden fruit from the Tree of Knowledge of Good and Evil. Eve, in turn, shared the fruit with Adam. Succumbing to temptation, both were expelled from the Garden of Eden. This act of disobedience marked a turning point in the relationship between humanity and the divine. As punishment for their sin, God placed two cherubim at the entrance of Eden with a flaming sword to prevent humanity from returning to the garden.

Thus, the serpent, later interpreted as Satan, played a crucial role in one of the Bible's most well-known and significant narratives. Its appearance in the Garden of Eden marked the beginning of a long history of temptation, sin, and redemption. In this earthly paradise, a being of twisted beauty and hidden wisdom stealthily slithered among the leaves and shadows. It was Satan, the fallen angel, who had taken on the form of a serpent.

Satan, in the guise of a serpent, silently approached Eve, the first woman, with a seductive whisper from its forked tongue. Its eyes flashed with forbidden knowledge, and its words were woven with tempting promises. It defied the one rule given by God: not to eat from the tree of the knowledge of good and evil.

Eve, enveloped in intrigue and seduced by hidden knowledge, found herself irresistibly drawn into the enigmatic conversation with that singular serpent. Her longing for wisdom, her insatiable ambition, led her to taste the forbidden fruit, and beside her, Adam also succumbed. In that moment, sin stealthily slipped into the world, and humanity fell into the shadows of knowledge, separated from divinity. The serpent played its role as tempter, and Satan, in his cunning form, achieved his revenge against divine creation.

In the crucible of the sin of knowledge, we reflect on the nature of our relentless curiosity. Are we prepared to unravel the mysteries that await us, or perhaps is the tireless pursuit of answers a divine punishment? As science and physics progress, each discovery seems to breed more questions than answers. Could this be our downfall and sin, trapped in an endless cycle of questioning?

In this modern era, we observe how powerful individuals and scientists sometimes play at being gods, pushing the limits of knowledge. At times, ignorance may be a sweet delight in life, as if by knowing everything, we lose the innocence and peace that simplicity of the unknown brings. Thus, as humanity persists in its unrestrained quest for understanding, the question arises: is our eagerness to know the source of our own downfall, or our liberation?

The story of Satan in the form of a serpent in the Garden of Eden is a story full of mystery and symbolism. It represents temptation, the fall and the introduction of sin into the world, as well as the complexity of human decisions. In my opinion this refers to the moment that humans stop acting like animals and questioning our environment and the burden that this entails, the fact of not being able to explain the meaning of our lives is reflected in the burden of knowledge. The figure of Satan as the cunning serpent remains a powerful symbol of the struggle between good and evil, wisdom and temptation in the narrative of the paranormal.

THE BOOK OF ENOCH

We refer to an ancient text that is part of apocryphal and pseudepigraphic literature. This book is attributed to Enoch, a biblical figure mentioned in Genesis as an antediluvian who walked with God before being taken to heaven. However, the Book of Enoch is considered by many scholars to be a work written long after the period in which the supposed author lived. The Book of Enoch consists of several components, with the most notable being the "Book of the Watchers" and the "Book of the Secrets of Enoch." These books present a narrative that includes visions, prophecies, and teachings on a wide range of subjects, including fallen angels, the genealogy of giants, divine judgment, and the nature of the cosmos.

The book contains unique material on the origins of demons and the Nephilim, who are the offspring of fallen angels and human women. It also explains why the Genesis flood was necessary to punish the rebellious angels and their descendants. Additionally, the book presents a prophetic vision of the Messiah's thousand-year reign.

It also provides an explanation of the origin and nature of evil spirits that tempted humanity and opposed God. The book influenced the idea that fallen angels will be chained in the abyss until the day of judgment. Moreover, the book inspired other authors to write similar works, such as the Second Book of Enoch, the Third Book of Enoch, and the Book of Jubilees.

"Book of the Watchers," offers a detailed narrative about the fallen angels and their interactions with humanity. These fallen angels are considered demons in many interpretations and play a prominent role in the work. Some examples of fallen angels mentioned in the Book of Enoch include: Azazel, Semyaza, Barakel, Gadreel, Shamhazai.

The Book of Enoch has been the subject of debate and controversy, and its authenticity and origin are topics of constant discussion among scholars. Despite its non-canonical status, it remains a text of interest to those exploring mystery, spirituality, and theology in the context of religious scriptures and ancient literature.

DEMONOLOGY

Demonology is the study of demons, those malevolent beings that lurk in the shadows and can possess or tempt humans. Demonology has its origins in ancient civilizations, where the existence of good and evil spirits influencing human fate was widely believed. As mentioned earlier, the Egyptians, Greeks, Persians, and Hindus had their own mythologies about these supernatural entities.

However, it was within the Judeo-Christian tradition that demonology gained greater prominence, considering demons as fallen angels who rebelled against God and were expelled from heaven. During the Middle Ages and the Renaissance, demonology developed as a branch of theology that attempted to classify and rank demons, as well as explain their origins, names, powers, and modes of operation. It also focused on combating them through exorcisms and rituals.

One of the most influential books of this era was the Malleus Maleficarum (The Hammer of Witches), written by two Dominican inquisitors in 1486. This work asserted the existence and power of witchcraft as a threat to the Catholic faith and offered methods to identify and prosecute witches, who were believed to be in league with the devil.

Demonology also played an important role in other religions, such as Islam, Buddhism, and Zoroastrianism, where the presence of an evil being opposed to God or goodness was also believed. In Islam, this being is called Shaytan or Iblis, in Buddhism, Mara, and in Zoroastrianism, Angra Mainyu.

Today, demonology remains a discipline that fascinates and terrifies many. Some consider it a science, others a superstition. Some practice it as a form of magic, others as a form of faith. The truth is that demons remain a mystery that defies our reason and our imagination.

SUCCUBUS FROM NIGHTMARE

Succubi and incubi are mysterious and seductive beings that have captivated the imagination of humanity for centuries. They are described as demons or spirits that are related to dreams and lust, and their origin dates back to the Middle Ages.

These beings, one female (succubus) and the other male (incubis), have been the focus of countless legends and stories.

Succubi: Succubi are generally represented as female figures of supernatural beauty. Their goal is to seduce men, often in dreams, and have sexual relations with them. Succubi are believed to feed on the sexual energy of their victims and can cause physical and emotional weakness. The idea of an encounter with a succubus can be both exciting and terrifying, raising questions of desire, temptation, and danger.

Incubi: Incubi are the male counterpart of succubi. It is believed that they seek to seduce women in their dreams, and are attributed with the ability to have sexual relations with them. Like succubi, incubi are considered evil beings that feed on the sexual energy of their victims. The idea of an incubus lurking in the dead of night is a source of mystery and fear in many cultures.

Belief in succubi and incubi is intertwined with the history of witchcraft and demonology in the Middle Ages. At that time, it was believed that nocturnal experiences of a sexual and erotic nature were caused by these demonic beings. The Catholic Church and civil authorities carried out persecutions and witch trials based on alleged interaction with succubi and incubi.

Today, these figures remain part of folklore and popular culture, and their existence is considered primarily in the realm of the paranormal and supernatural. Succubi and incubi represent the tension between desire and fear, between attraction and danger, and remain enigmatic elements in the rich tradition of the mysterious and the unknown.

EXORCISMOR

One of the most notorious cases is the case of Anneliese Michel, a young German woman who died in 1976 after undergoing 67 exorcism sessions over 10 months. Anneliese suffered from epileptic attacks and depression since her adolescence, and became convinced that she was possessed by several demons. Some of the symptoms he presented were hallucinations, aversion to religious objects, self-harm, superhuman strength and guttural voices. Anneliese's parents requested permission from the Catholic Church to perform an exorcism, which was granted by the bishop of Würzburg. Two priests were in charge of practicing the ritual, which was recorded on audio tapes. In them you can hear Anneliese scream, blaspheme, pray and name the demons that tormented her: Lucifer, Judas, Nero, Cain, Hitler and others.

On July 1, 1976, Anneliese died from malnutrition and starvation, weighing only 30 kilograms. Her parents and the priests were accused of negligent homicide and sentenced to six months in prison with probation.

Another case is that of Roland Doe, an American teenager who inspired the famous movie The Exorcist. Roland was a lonely and shy boy living in Maryland in 1949. After the death of his aunt Harriet, a spiritualist who had taught him to use a Ouija board, Roland began to experience strange phenomena in his house: inexplicable noises, objects moving on their own, scratches on the walls and on his body. His parents took him to several doctors and psychiatrists, but no logical explanation was found. Finally, they turned to the Catholic Church, which authorized an exorcism. Father Edward Hughes was tasked with performing it, but had to stop when Roland cut his arm with a piece of the mattress. The case was moved to St. Louis, where two Jesuit priests, William Bowdern and Walter Halloran, continued the exorcism for several weeks. According to their testimonies, Roland showed signs of possession such as levitation, voice changes, speaking unknown languages, and marks on his skin with words like "evil" or "sin." On April 18, 1949, after more than 30 sessions, the priests managed to free Roland from the demon with the help of a crucifix and a medal of Saint Michael the Archangel.

Lastly, we have one of the most controversial and fascinating cases in the history of demonic possession. Julia, a middle-aged woman from the United States, hardworking and independent, found herself trapped in a supernatural struggle after participating in several demonic rituals.

Raised in a Catholic family, Julia drifted away from her beliefs and became interested in the paranormal, eventually associating with satanic sects or groups. After participating in these rituals, she began to feel attacked by supernatural forces and sought help from the Catholic Church.

Dr. Richard E. Gallagher, a renowned and respected psychiatrist in the United States and an associate professor at New York Medical College, was contacted to evaluate Julia. What he observed during psychiatric consultations and exorcism sessions defied all logic.

Julia could speak foreign languages with perfect fluency, languages she had never known or studied. Her voice would change, sounding masculine and guttural. She had an impressive gift of clairvoyance, able to accurately describe places, illnesses, homes, names, and even situations involving team members and their families. She exhibited supernatural strength, and sudden temperature changes would occur at the exorcism site. Objects in the room, including shelves, would fly around. But undoubtedly, the most impressive phenomenon was Julia's levitation; on one occasion, she remained suspended above the ground for 30 continuous minutes. Additionally, a documentary titled "The Devil's Trial" explores this case in depth and presents real recordings of this supposed demonic possession.

However, it is important to note that, although these phenomena were documented by respected professionals, the interpretation of these events is subject to debate. Some firmly believe in the reality of demonic possessions, while others view these phenomena as manifestations of mental illnesses or neurological disorders.

Therefore, although there is documented evidence of Julia's case, whether this evidence is evidence of true demonic possession or not depends largely on the personal beliefs of the individual. This case challenges our understanding of the world and leads us to question the thin line that separates the natural from the supernatural. What mysteries still await us in the shadows? Only time will tell.

Vatican Secret Archives

As a researcher of the paranormal world, one cannot help but feel fascinated by the enigmatic "Vatican Secret Archives," formally known as the "Vatican Apostolic Archives." These archives contain a vast amount of historical documents, papal correspondence, and records of the Catholic Church dating back centuries, and access to them is restricted to the public.

The Vatican Secret Archives are renowned for their secrecy and for housing a wealth of information that has intrigued paranormal researchers for decades. Among this extensive collection of historical documents, there are cases and events that defy any logical explanation. Although access to these archives is difficult, there have been leaks and accounts suggesting the presence of solid evidence of paranormal events and inexplicable phenomena.

One of the most notable cases is the "Demon of Loudun." This is one of the most famous and terrifying cases in the history of demonic possessions. It all began in 1634 in the small French town of Loudun. The Ursuline nuns of the local convent started exhibiting signs of demonic possession. Urbain Grandier, the parish priest of St-Pierre-du-Marche in Loudun, was accused of being responsible for these possessions. Grandier was an attractive and refined man who had had relationships with several women in the locality. Due to his behavior, Grandier had numerous enemies in the town of Loudun. In 1629, Grandier had a confrontation with Jacques de Thibault, an agent of Cardinal Richelieu, which led to the agent physically assaulting the priest.

Grandier marched to Paris to denounce Thibault before King Louis XIII; in turn, his enemies accused him of immorality before his ecclesiastical superior, the Bishop of Poitiers, Henri-Louis Chasteignier de la Rochepozay.

In Loudun, an investigation into Grandier's conduct was carried out, led by one of his main enemies, prosecutor Louis Trincant. On November 15, 1629, Grandier was arrested in Poitiers by order of the bishop. On March 3, 1630, he was sentenced to abstain from performing his ecclesiastical duties for five years in the diocese of Poitiers, and for the rest of his life in the city of Loudun.

The Ursuline convent in Loudun had been founded in 1626. Since the following year, its superior was Mother Jeanne des Anges. By 1634, seventeen nuns, including the superior, lived in the convent. The superior had requested Grandier to become the confessor of the nuns, but Grandier had declined her request. After Grandier's refusal, the position was accepted by Canon Mignon, Grandier's rival in the ecclesiastical career.

The nuns of the Ursuline convent in Loudun claimed to be possessed by demons and accused Father Grandier of being responsible for their possessions. This scandal attracted the attention of the Church and civil authorities, and Grandier was subjected to a trial heavily influenced by the collective hysteria and politics of the time.

Ultimately, Urban Grandier was accused of witchcraft and sentenced to die at the stake. Before that, his legs were broken. The parish priest died at the stake on August 18, 1634, at the age of 44.

This case was so impactful that it inspired numerous literary and cinematic works. Aldous Huxley published a novel based on this true event called "The Devils of Loudun" in 1952. The story is a detailed examination of the events where Urbain Grandier was accused and condemned for witchcraft and seduction of the nuns at the convent.

Historical records and Church documents from that time, housed in the Vatican Secret Archives, detail the exorcisms and supernatural events that baffled witnesses. Paranormal researchers suggest these records provide solid evidence of the existence of paranormal phenomena.

Besides the "Demon of Loudun," the Vatican Secret Archives have also been linked to miraculous events, prophecies, and mystical revelations that, according to some, defy logical explanation. These ancient documents have fueled the imagination of those seeking answers in the paranormal world and have led to speculation about the hidden knowledge and secrets guarded by the Catholic Church. Although the Church has made strides in opening some of these archives, much of their content remains a mystery.

DEMONS

Now that I have your attention, let me warn you: there is no turning back. Your mind is about to open a door that may be difficult to close. In the pages of this illustrative dictionary, I will present to you a gallery of demonic entities like you have never seen before. Accompanied by vivid illustrations and the most complete information, these malevolent creatures will transport you to a world of mystery and darkness. Each demon is an enigma, a manifestation of the uncanny in its most intriguing form. Prepare to enter an abyss of knowledge and terror, where curiosity will guide you through the deepest paths of panic... ---...

Aamon: Also known as Amon in the shadowy chronicles of demonology, stands as a marquis in the infernal realms, commanding forty legions of sinister entities. His dominion extends across the boundaries of time, as he possesses the power to unravel the secrets of the past and foresee future destinies, acting as a guardian of shadows who untangles the threads of time. In the demonic hierarchy, he is regarded as a loyal servant of Astaroth and a pillar of allegiance in the service of Satanachia. His name, "Aamon," whispers promises of wealth and greed, drawing those with an insatiable appetite for power and material possessions. This demon is intrinsically linked to the cardinal sin of wrath.

Aamon rules the infernal pacts, granting those who have made agreements with Satan himself the gift of glimpses into the destiny and true nature of their allies and enemies. Its manifestations are changing and elusive.

Occasionally appearing as a man with the head of an owl or as a hybrid creature with the head of a wolf and a snake's tail. Other times, it takes the form of a wolf that breathes fire from its mouth or a being with the head of a crow and the teeth of a dog. His figure is blurred in the darkness, always in constant transformation, wrapped in a cloak of mystery and darkness.

It is speculated that its origin can be found in Egyptian deities, particularly in the god Amun, whose name carries the heavy burden of the oppression suffered by the Jewish people under the yoke of the ancient Egyptian Empire. Furthermore, Aamon is ominously associated with Ba'al Hammon, the Carthaginian deity whose name ominously evokes "He Who Incites Wrath and Murder." These connotations only serve to stoke the fear it arouses.

Abalám: Known as Abalán, he is a lesser-known prince of Hell, part of the court and retinue of King Paymón. He takes the form of a woman crowned with a diadem sparkling with precious stones. Abalám commands two hundred legions of rebellious angels and infernal forces.

Abadón: Whose name also echoes in Greek as Apollyon, is an enigmatic figure found in the pages of the Bible, a being who traverses the realms of the divine and the infernal. His mystery intertwines with two fundamental meanings. In the Old Testament, Abadón is described as an unfathomable abyss, a dark chasm generally associated with the world of the dead, Sheol. This concept casts a shadow over the threshold between life and death, a place where the secrets of the beyond remain hidden.

However, in the Book of Revelation in the New Testament, Abadón takes on a different form. Here, he is mentioned as the leader of an army of apocalyptic locusts, an angel of great power. The text transcribes his name from Hebrew into Greek characters, revealing: "whose name in Hebrew is Abadón," and translates it as "which in Greek means Apollyon."

The Vulgate adds an unnecessary note, which in Latin translates as "Destroyer." The duality of Abaddon is intriguing: some see him as one of the most important generals in the Empire of Darkness, while others consider him a divine representative, holder of the key to the abyss and leader of the plague of locusts that will be unleashed upon the enemies of God at the End of Time. Their true intentions and their role in the cosmic tapestry remain shrouded in mystery, defying all attempts at complete understanding.

Abducius: Demon who uprooted enormous trees and crushed men with them.

Abduxuel: One of the ruling demons of the lunar mansions, according to the tradition of Enoch.

Abrahel: Demon who is dedicated to seducing the poor in spirit, especially peasants and people with little education, always taking the appearance of a beautiful and willing woman; Its purpose is to recruit Devil worshipers on Earth.

ABADDON

Abraxas: (Abrasax and Abracax): Greek god who is believed to represent Good and Evil in a single entity.

Abyss: Its name means 'desperate'

Acatriel: One of the three princes of good demons (in the Hebrew Kabbalah, which admits demons of two kinds).

Acham: Demon of a lower order, which is conjured on Thursdays.

Aclahayir: A spirit and genius of the fourth hour of the Nuctemeron.

Adonis (Adón, Dumuzi, and Tammuz): Known as 'lord' or 'master', Adonis is a Phoenician demon associated with pyromania, presiding over fires.

Adirael: A demon under the command of Beelzebub.

Adriel: One of the demons of the lunar mansions, according to Enochian tradition.

Af: A minor demon in Hebrew mythology, characterized by a ram's head; originating from Nubia and Abyssinia.

Agagliareth (also known as Agaliarept and Agliaret): A great general of Hell, commanding the second legion. He possesses the power to uncover all secrets and holds dominion over Europe and Asia Minor. He commands Buer, Gusoyn, and Botis.

Agares: Emerges as a powerful duke of the underworld, ruling with a firm hand over thirty-one legions of demons. Once a member of the order of Virtues before his fall, Agares' descent exemplifies the profound fall of the rebellious angels. His abilities are as deep as the abysses he inhabits. Agares can compel fugitives to return, unleash earthquakes that shake the very foundations of reality, and teach forgotten languages. He particularly delights in spreading immoral and forbidden expressions.

Agares' abilities are as unfathomable as the abysses he inhabits. He has the gift of making fugitives return, triggering earthquakes that shake the foundations of reality and teaching forgotten languages, revealing a peculiar pleasure in spreading immoral and forbidden expressions. Grimoires, such as the Ars Goetia and the Pseudomonarchia daemonum, have immortalized his name in the chronicles of the supernatural. His form manifests as that of an old man riding on a crocodile, with a majestic falcon perched on his fist. It is rumored that Agares is under the command of Lucífugo Rofocale, a detail that sheds more enigmas about his nature and his role in the dark designs of the underworld.

AGARES SEAL

Alecto: One of the three avenging Greek Furies of Tartarus. The Furies are female entities that dwell in Tartarus and are associated with vengeance and punishment.

Alocer: Also known in various forms as Allocen, Alloces, he emerges as an enigmatic demon whose records intertwine within the channels of demonology. This being, mentioned in grimoires that explore the depths of the underworld, such as the Liber Officiorum Spirituum, the Pseudomonarchia Daemonum, and the Lemegeton Clavicula Salomonis, evokes both curiosity and fear.

In the Lemegeton Clavicula Salomonis, Alocer stands as the fifty-second spirit, while in the Pseudomonarchia Daemonum he is listed as the sixty-third spirit, a great duke of the inferno. His appearance is astonishing, taking the form of a soldier with the head of a lion, whose roars ignite flames, and he rides majestically, often on dragon's legs. His mysterious duties include teaching astronomy and the liberal arts, as well as granting familiars. It is rumored that he commands 36 legions of demons at his will. In the Liber Officiorum Spirituum, Alocer appears as Allogor or Algor, once again under the title of great duke, albeit with a completely different appearance and abilities.

he manifests as a knight with a lance, offering answers to the deepest questions and cunning advice for Machiavellian plans. Only thirty legions of demons bow to his authority. Alocer appears dressed as a knight, riding a huge horse; his figure resembles the features of a lion; he has a flushed complexion and fiery eyes; he speaks gravely. It is said that he makes those he protects happy in their families. An enigmatic and complex being, Alocer continues to baffle and attract those who venture into his mysterious domain.

ALOCER

Algol: In the dark pages of Arabic astrology, Algol emerges as an intriguing spirit. This celestial demon, associated with the most sinister stars, captivates the attention of Eastern astrologers who seek to unravel its cosmic mysteries. Its influence is woven into the threads of destiny, suggesting an enigmatic power that fascinates those who explore the secrets of the firmament.

Allatou: Personifies temptation and seduction. She is the consort of Nergal, and her presence whispers in the ears of mortals, leading them toward morally ambiguous paths. Allatou becomes the shadow that envelops the darkest desires, playing her subtle yet persuasive role in the fabric of morality and immorality.

Alpiel: Manifests as a demon of modest rank, his indolent and bucolic nature intertwined with the essence of protecting fruit trees. This being, though less imposing compared to his infernal counterparts, demonstrates that even in the dark realms there are entities that find their purpose in the guardianship of nature and its gifts.

Alricaus: The dark dance of invocations reaches its climax on Saturdays when Alricaus, a strategic demon, emerges to lead the infernal legions under his command. A war chief and sage, Alricaus rules over 22 legions of devils. His gift for teaching logic and psychology to those who serve him reveals an unusually educational aspect among demons, challenging expectations and immersing those who invoke him in infernal learning.

Aluca: The enigmatic figure of Aluca, also known as Alouqua, presents herself as a shadowy succubus. This female demon, with her vampiric nature, delights in draining men, insinuating her dark charms to push them to their limits. Her nefarious influence leads her victims into an abyss of despair, guiding them towards the tragic fate of suicide

Alukah: Among the infernal entities that slip through the folds of Hebrew mythology, the unsettling figure of Alukah emerges, with roots tracing back to ancient Babylon. This being, lurking in the darkness of the night, feeds on the vital essence of unsuspecting sleepers. By sucking the blood of its victims, Alukah weaves a web of mystery and terror, leaving a trail of anguish in its nocturnal wake.

Amane: In the pantheon of celestial rebellion, Amane stands out as one of the 200 angels who defied divine will under Samyaza's leadership. His descent to Earth marked a pivotal shift as he joined humankind, sharing with them the sciences forbidden by the divine. Amane became a bearer of forbidden knowledge, challenging established limits and sowing the seeds of rebellion.

Amazarac: One of the 200 rebellious angels who descended from Heaven, Amazarac taught humans all the secrets of witchcraft and enchantments.

Amdusias: In the dark recesses of demonology, Amdusias emerges as an enigmatic being holding the title of Grand Duke, commanding thirty legions of loyal followers (though some authors suggest the number is 29). His appearance is as perplexing as his power, often described as a human with claws instead of hands and feet.

the head of a unicorn rising majestically. But the most intriguing thing is his trumpet, a symbol of his voice, a voice that is said to be so powerful that it can unleash storms.

Amdusias is linked to thunder, and it is said that his voice echoes in the roar of storms. According to ancient legends, this demon, when summoned, can offer otherworldly musical concerts, although no one will be able to witness its presence. Their music, accompanied by the sound of trumpets, is capable of bending the trees at will, creating a symphony that resonates in the realm of the supernatural. In the labyrinth of demonology, Amdusias stands as a mystery that awaits those brave or foolish who dare to invoke his power. His legacy is inscribed in Johann Weyer's Pseudomonarchia Daemonum (1583), a chronicle of dark beings who, like Amdusias, continue to intrigue and seduce those who dare to explore their enigmatic domain.

SEAL OF AMDUSIAS

Amoymon, also known as Amaimon and Amoimon: Is an infernal king and prince in the Eastern demonic hierarchy. He is summoned at two intervals: in the morning from 9 to 12, and in the afternoon from 3 to 6. He manifests surrounded by flames and possesses knowledge in astrology and the liberal arts. Additionally, he can reveal treasures hidden by other demons to his followers. He commands 36 legions of fallen angels and Powers, with Asmoda (or Asmodeus) serving as his lieutenant, the first prince of his domains.

Anamelech, also known as Anamalech: His name means 'good king.' He is a dark demon, bearer of bad news; when he becomes visible, he takes the form of a partridge, often showing his presence by throwing objects like silver pellets or coins. One can hear him whispering the bad news he carries at night. He is an omen of divine punishment for offenses or lies for personal gain. He was worshipped in Sepharvaim (Assyria). Some demonologists argue that this devil represents the Moon, just as Adramelech represents the Sun.

Anazareth, also known as Anazarel: Is a demon tasked with guarding underground treasures. Alongside Gaziel and Fecor, he shakes the foundations of houses, stirs up storms, rings bells at midnight, makes specters appear, and inspires nocturnal terrors. His stigma is that he cannot know love.

Andromalius: An infernal count who can return both the thief and the stolen goods, punish thieves and other wicked people, and uncover hidden treasures.

Aneberg, also known as Anabergo and Anneberg: Is a German demon, appearing either as a goat with golden horns or as a gigantic horse with a large neck, who lives underground and lacks any kind traits It is the terror of the miners, since many of of them die upon contact with its horrible breath.

Anubis: The Egyptian god of death and lord of the underworld (Fifth Dynasty), son of Set and Nephthys, with the head of a jackal or hawk. Patron of embalmers, he guided souls to be judged regarding their future.

Any: Among the shadows of the underworld, Any rises as the demon presiding over the infernal realms. His imposing figure and dominion over condemned souls make him a feared entity, ruling with authority over torment and perdition.

Acheron: In Greek mythology, Acheron stands as a demon-river flowing through the underworld. This cursed stream has a unique peculiarity: no one has the privilege of crossing its waters more than once. Acheron thus becomes the insurmountable barrier separating the world of the living from the dark realm of the dead, enforcing its law with unyielding rigor.

Aquiel: He emerges as a demon invoked in the dark rites of Sunday midnight, preferably in deserted places. This infernal being demands the darkness of the new moon or the celestial cover of storm clouds as a backdrop for his conjuring. In exchange for his presence, Aquiel requests a singular offering: a hair plucked from the head, symbolizing a dark pact and a connection to the deepest secrets of the underworld.

Arachula: In the air laden with malevolence, Arachula manifests as an evil spirit dancing among the currents of the wind.

Araic, also known as Arakho: Among the dark legends, Araic stands as a demon who challenges the boundaries of time. Also known as Arakho, this infernal being plunges into the epic battle against the Sun and the Moon. His nefarious mission centers on seizing the divine elixir, the wine of immortality, unleashing cosmic conflicts as he seeks to deprive eternity of its divine nectar. In this celestial confrontation, Araic weaves a tale of cosmic struggles and diabolical ambitions.

Ardad: He emerges as a sinister guide lurking in the shadows. This demon, with cunning and malice, becomes the conductor of lost travelers, leading them down tortuous paths to unknown destinations. His influence is felt in moments of confusion and disorientation, where his presence manifests as a treacherous shadow steering the lost toward unfamiliar and dangerous terrains.

Ariel: In Hebrew mythology, a demonic spirit of the air (more specifically of the winds). In Islam, he is an archangel of God, depicted as a man with a lion's face.

Arioc: In the demonic firmament of vengeance, Arioc rises as an implacable entity. This demon, woven into the shadows of mythology, embodies the very essence of retribution. In his presence, anger becomes a dark art, and retribution a sinister dance. As the executor of vengeance, Arioc awakens in the depths of human consciousness, reminding us of the consequences of crossing certain boundaries and unleashing the darkest forces of infernal reprisal.

Arioch: One of the fallen angels who was punished for following Satan's rebellion.

Asmodeus: This demon is woven with threads of lust and mystery. In the Book of Tobit, he is depicted as a vengeful spirit, tearing apart marital bonds over seven wedding nights. However, a glimmer of hope appears in the figure of Tobias, who, with the guidance of the archangel Raphael, initiates an intriguing confrontation. The chosen weapon? A fish, whose red-hot entrails produce a smoke potent enough to suffocate the demon himself.

In Jewish legends, Asmodeus takes on a different hue. He is described as a character involved in a pact with King Solomon, destined to build the majestic Temple of Jerusalem. Other narratives have him assuming Solomon's identity for years, creating a web of mystery that spans different dimensions. A king among demons, a banished lover, and a figure who fathers innumerable demon progeny dance in the shadows of his mythology.

He is also attributed with being the father of the wizard Merlin, who often appears in tales of occultism and magic.

In the darker tableau of the Middle Ages, Asmodeus is pinpointed as the architect of lust, embodying one of the seven deadly sins. An intriguing figure in the vast panoply of demons, Asmodeus emanates an aura of mystery that twists through time and cultures, enduring in the shadowy recesses of mythology.

ASMODEO

Asmoug, also known as Aschmog: A demon from Persia, Asmoug sows discord, quarrels, and disputes under the orders of Ahriman. He is depicted as a hellish serpent with two legs, spawning all venomous creatures.

Astaroth: The enigmatic figure of Astaroth unfolds as a dark and seductive puzzle. In the realms of demonology, he rises as the Grand Duke of Hell, forming a shadowy trinity with Beelzebub and Lucifer. His mysterious connection to the Near Eastern goddess Astarte adds an intriguing layer to his identity.

His tale intertwines with betrayal and downfall; once a seraph and Prince of the Order of Thrones, his descent into the abyss sparked a storm of controversies. Was his fall forged by human temptation or a dark design of higher realms? The question lingers like an echo in the corners of mystery. Despite his fall into darkness, Astaroth whispers with an untainted voice, asserting his purity in a sea of sin and deceit, defying the conventions of his own fall.

According to the Pseudomonarchia Daemonum (1577), he appears in the form of a tainted angel, seated on an infernal dragon and holding a viper in his left hand. It is advised that the summoner approaches with a magical ring to withstand his pestilent breath. In the illustrated edition of the Dictionnaire Infernal (1818), he is depicted as a naked man with feathered wings, crowned, holding a serpent in one hand and riding a creature with dragon wings and a serpent tail. Sixteenth-century demonologists noted that his attacks against men are most potent in August.

His adversary is Saint Bartholomew, who protects him since he resisted his temptations. For others, it teaches mathematics and crafts, can make men invisible, lead them to hidden treasures, and answer any question asked of it. It was also said that it could give mortals powers over snakes. According to Francis Barret (d. C. 1801), he is the prince of accusers and inquisitors.

ASTAROTH ILLUSTRATION

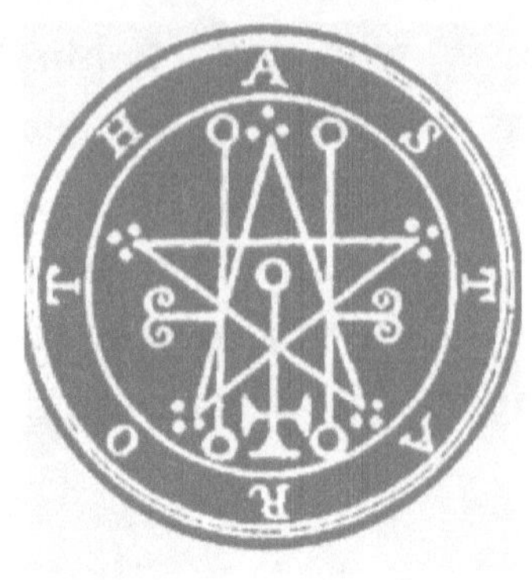

Astarté, also known as Baalit, Astartea, Estarot, and Diana: Queen of the spirits of death and consort of Astaroth, Astarté presides over the pleasures of love. She is depicted with the head of a calf with horns and a cross in her hand. She bore two children: Desire and Love.

Athatriel: A fallen angel, condemned for siding neither with God nor with Lucifer.

Até: A malevolent Greek deity, daughter of Zeus and Eris (discord), Até personified vengeance, injustice, perversity, fatality, and the inherent evil of human nature or the rashness and folly of thoughtlessness. She once resided on Mount Olympus but was cast out for sowing discord. Subtle and ethereal, she never touched the ground, always hovering above the heads of men to inspire them toward evil. Her abstract and vengeful nature recalls that of Erinys and Nemesis.

Átropos: The eldest of the three Greek Fates (or Moirai), daughters of Zeus and Themis, who governed the destinies of mortals. Átropos was responsible for cutting the thread of life.

Avang Dhu: Meaning "black beaver," Avang Dhu is a Celtic demon, destroyer of the demiurge's work (the universal creative power), often depicted in the form of a dragon.

Azaradel: One of the demons under the command of Samael, Azazel, and Samyaza, who educated humans about the knowledge of the Moon and its influence on Creation.

Azahel: An alluring and seductive demon, Azahel taught women the arts of makeup and cosmetics. He was one of the angels who rebelled against God under the leadership of Azazel and Samyaza. It is said that he is chained upon sharp rocks in a dark desert, awaiting the Final Judgment.

Azazel: A name that resonates through the pages of ancient rituals and scriptures. In the biblical context, it is entwined with the mysterious rite of the Day of Atonement, where two goats are chosen, one for Yavé and the other for Azazel. This name evokes intriguing symbolism.

Within certain traditions of Judaism and Christianity, Azazel becomes a fallen angel, a being whose story is interwoven with the fall of rebellious angels and their banishment to the underworld. However, in rabbinic interpretations, he is not an entity but rather translates literally to "The Lord of the Goats," suggesting a profound connection with the scapegoat sent into the desert during the Day of Atonement. This goat carries the people's sins, purifying the Tabernacle and ultimately weaving a tapestry of mystery around Azazel.

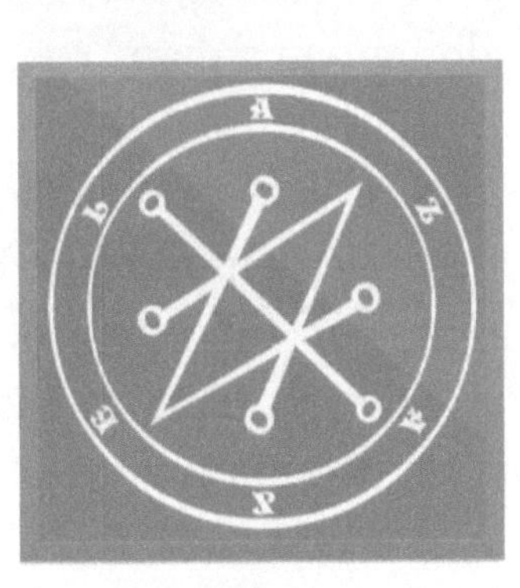

AZAZEL SEAL

Azebel: A second-order demon in Hebrew mythology.

Azhi Dahaka, also known as Azi Dahaka, Azi Dahak, Dahaka, and Dahak: A demonic figure from Zoroastrian Persia.

Azlat: A demon from Hebrew mythology.

Azrael, also known as Ezrael, Izra'il, Izrafil, Abu-Jahia, and Abou-Jaria: In Islam, the Angel of Death; in Hebrew demonology, an Archangel. He was Lucifer's lieutenant during the rebellion. Azrael is said to be covered with a million veils, towering above the heavens, with the entire world resting in his hands like a plate from which he can consume as he pleases. He possesses four faces: one at the front, one atop his head, one at the back, and one beneath his feet. He has four wings, and his body is covered in countless eyes; each time one closes, a human soul perishes.

Baal, also known as Beel and Bel: A deity (likely representing the sun) worshiped by various ancient peoples of Asia Minor, including the Phoenicians, Chaldeans, Babylonians, Sidonians, and Israelites. He has the power to render those who invoke him invisible and can bestow wisdom upon a man.

Bael: The cunning king of the underworld, whose name echoes through the shadowy recesses of mythology and demonology. He stands as the first among the monarchs of the inferno, a formidable infernal power mentioned in ancient grimoires like the Ars Goetia and the Pseudomonarchia Daemonum.

Bael embodies the might of the East, a figure reminiscent of the ancient Baal. For ages, Bael has served as the personal assistant to Satan.

A position that places him at the top. His reign spans legions of demons, with numbers varying depending on sources, ranging between 66 and 72 legions, with an impressive total of 456,000 demons under his command. Its power is whispered to intensify in the month of October, reaching its peak on the holiday of Samhain, when the veils between the worlds are blurred.

BAEL ILLUSTRATION

Despite his demonic nature, Bael is characterized by his wisdom and directness. His personality, sober and direct, surprises with its friendly insight, and although he does not lie, his mystery remains unfathomable. The king of the underworld, an enigmatic figure that provokes fascination and fear in equal measure.

BAEL SEAL

Baalcephon, also known as Baalzephon, Balcephon, and Baal-Sefon: A deity of Egyptian origin. He serves as the captain of the guards and sentinels of Hell; later on, he took on the role of overseeing the loyalty of slaves.

Baalzebub: The Phoenician god of oracles; a second-tier demon.

Bacchus, also known as Iacchus: His name originates from the Indo-European term that gave rise to the Sanskrit baksha ('to devour'); from the Greek bakchos, symbolizing the fire that consumes sacrifices. He is often seen presiding over the Sabbath.

Bacon: Known as the demon of jealousy; naturally malevolent and resentful, he is the one who sows discord between lovers.

Bahaman: Unlike his chaotic counterparts, this demon stands as a peacemaker in the realm of overwhelming emotions. His essence lies in soothing the wrath that consumes tormented souls.

Baltazo: An incubus demon of great seduction, known only for possessing women to engage in sexual relations, as no other occupation is attributed to him.

Baphomet: A figure shrouded in mystery and controversy, whose name alone can send chills down the spine of those who dare to venture into its dark domain.

Depicted as a grotesque creature, often described as a hybrid being between a goat and a human, with wings and twisted horns that reach towards the sky, Baphomet embodies the macabre and the unknown. Although his origin is uncertain and he has been intertwined with legends and myths throughout the ages, Baphomet has come to symbolize the occult and the hermetic.

SEAL OF BAPHOMET

In popular culture, his terrifying image is commonly associated with Satanism and demonic cults. His eyes, often described as piercing and challenging, seem to read the souls of those who observe him, leaving an eerie sense that Baphomet is much more than just a representation.

This name, almost whispered in esoteric circles, has been the subject of endless debates and speculations that shroud the figure in an even denser veil of mystery. Among the theories that weave together like strands of a spell, some suggest that "Baphomet" is an arcanely coded word, while others posit the possibility that it is an intricate anagram that holds deep meanings, only unravelable by minds initiated into the darkest secrets. Even the name itself, "Baphomet", has been the subject of speculation and conspiracy theories, adding a layer of mystery to this entity.

Some claim it is a coded word or anagram with hidden and deeper meanings. Whatever the truth behind Baphomet, his image lingers in the realm of terror and the unknown, inviting the curious to delve into the shadows and explore what lies beyond the threshold of reality.

BAPHOMET

Barbatos: One of Astaroth's three helper demons.

Barbelo: Demon of great power. He enjoys dominating men and exploits their weaknesses, such as lust and jealousy.

Barbudo, also known as Barqu and Barbu: A demon possessing the secret of the Philosopher's Stone, he appears in human form, his face covered by a massive, white beard.

Barkai: A lesser-ranking demon; he holds the secrets of the stars and was the master of astrologers.

Baron: His name derives from the Celtic baran or barwn, meaning 'Lord'. This demon was offered the hands and hearts of sacrificed children. Gilles de Rais was a devoted follower of the Baron, from whom he would obtain the recipe for the Philosopher's Stone.

Barrabam, also known as Barrabas: A high-ranking demon whose name was often engraved on magical rings and amulets.

Batscumbasa, also known as Batscun Bassa and Batscum-Pacha: A Turkish demon invoked to bring good weather or rain; he has a great fondness for bread, which he cannot find in Hell, so one must offer him generous amounts to gain his favor.

Bayemon: A king in the West, whose name appears in certain grimoires; he wields power over Passiel and Rosus.

Bebal, also known as Babeal and Babael: A demon who holds the rank of prince and serves as the guardian of graves.

Bechard: The Lord of Winds and Storms; he causes hail, rain, and disperses thunder through the power of a curse that includes crushed toads among other elements.

Bechet: A Friday demon with a peculiar fondness for nuts; he is a nocturnal spirit.

Behemoth: A demon from Hebrew mythology, a fierce enemy of Leviathan. According to legend, they clashed at the dawn of time and must be destroyed by God before they annihilate His Creation. It is also said that they will battle once again on Judgment Day.

Bel: The supreme deity of Chaldeo-Babylonian theogony, later transformed into a demon with a distinct, thunderous voice.

Beelzebub: The Lord of the Flies, a demonic entity that stands as a figure of darkness and terror. Merely uttering his name seems to invoke a sense of dread, as if calling upon him could cast a curse on those who dare. His origins trace back to the Philistine demon Baal-Zebub, a pagan idol linked to disease and misfortune. In his demonic form, Beelzebub has been depicted as a winged creature or even a malevolent god, with an appearance as grotesque as his deeds. This prince of darkness is notorious for leading humanity into corruption and decadence. He is considered one of Satan's chief aides and, in certain traditions, is even portrayed as the "Lord of Hell." The mere mention of his name has instilled fear throughout history, and he is often credited as the dark inspiration behind William Golding's literary masterpiece, Lord of the Flies, a portrayal of civilization's collapse into chaos and anarchy.

Beelzebub embodies the darkest aspects of humanity—temptation and perversion—lurking in the shadows, ever ready to corrupt unsuspecting souls.

Her sinister influence spreads like a cloak of darkness over all who venture into her realm. In her eyes, the darkest secrets and deepest temptations lurk, waiting for the right moment to emerge and drag souls down to doom. A single glance from her can inspire nightmares, and her name is a constant echo of fear and despair in the world of the occult.

SEAL AND ILLUSTRATION OF BEELZEBUB

Belial: The Prince of Lies, is a demonic figure who embodies deceitful seduction and corruption. His name resonates like a sinister echo in the shadows of the occult, and his malign influence runs deep in demonic legends. He is known as one of the Seven Princes of Hell and is a master in the art of betrayal and manipulation.

Belial's image is forged with cunning and malevolence. He is depicted as a being of deceptive beauty, with seductive features that hide his true nature. He is the master of false promises and temptations that cloud the minds of mortals. His words are like poison, weaving a web of deceit around him. This demon is not only a cunning deceiver, but also an instigator of discord and rebellion. His name is often associated with chaos and anarchy, and he is said to lead legions of demons in a realm of perversion and depravity.

ILLUSTRATION OF
BELIAL

SEAL OF BELIAL

Belias: A demon of great power, known as the Prince of Virtues.

Belphegor: An infamous entity that has haunted religious beliefs for centuries. Its origins are intertwined with ancient pagan deities, but over time, this being transformed into a malevolent demon, embodying depravity and corruption. The name Belphegor carries the echo of a dark past, linked to the worship of the Canaanite god Baal Pe'or.

In ancient texts, this demon is depicted as a figure associated with indecency and excess. His name, derived from the Hebrew word meaning "opening," is a harbinger of the obscenities and impious acts attributed to him.

The legend of Belphegor is steeped in nudity, excrement, and fornication, painting a vivid picture of impiety that is hard to forget. It is said that the worship of Baal Pe'or involved profane acts before this idol, a grotesque practice that revealed the basest aspects of humanity.

Christian exegetes and early theologians regarded Belphegor as an agent of evil, an enemy of virtuous souls. Over the centuries, demonology expanded with detailed descriptions of demons, including Belphegor. These dark accounts chronicled names, appearances, and the terrifying traits of these infernal beings. Through magical and esoteric literature, teachings on how to summon these malevolent spirits emerged. Belphegor and his sinister companions became the source of countless spells and forbidden rituals seeking power at any cost. At the crossroads of pagan mythology and religion, Belphegor remains a dark and frightening figure, whose hidden secrets continue to disturb the minds of those who dare to explore his legacy of corruption.

BELPHEGOR ILLUSTRATION

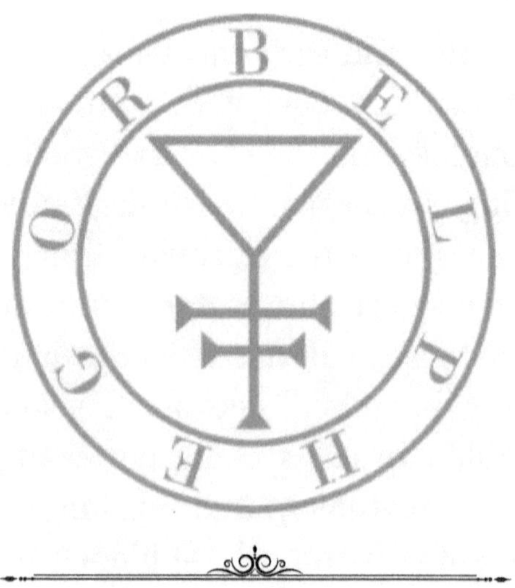

BELPHEGOR SEAL

Beng, also known as Bheng: His name stems from the Indo-European term that gave rise to the Sanskrit bheka, meaning 'frog'. He is the demon of the Gypsies, whose followers are snake worshippers, generally holding a deep respect for reptiles.

Bentameleon: A possessive devil, yet polite and well-mannered, who would even ask permission and offer himself to enter a body.

Bohinum: His name comes from the Hebrew bohu, meaning 'desolation'. In Hebrew mythology, he is the demon of evil. Additionally, this is the name given to an Armenian idol made of black metal, a symbol of the night.

Braathwaate: With his subtle malevolence, Braathwaate whispers doubts and confusion, shrouding human minds in a veil of misinformation.

Brifault, also known as Brifot, Briffaut, and Biffant: A powerful demon, often involved in acts of possession. Despite being little known, he is a legion commander.

Brulefer: A demon invoked when one desires to inspire lust, guaranteeing success in any erotic adventure.

Bucon: A demon of hatred, of the most vile kind, mentioned in the Clavicles of Solomon.

Buer: In the infernal realm, Buer, a demon of profound knowledge and power, rules with an iron hand. He presides over the second order of Hell, commanding fifty legions of demons. When the Sun resides in the constellation of Sagittarius, Buer emerges from the shadows, showcasing his wisdom and dark arts.

This demon has a peculiar nature, akin to Chiron, the central figure of Greek mythology who was half-man, half-horse. Buer, like his mythological counterpart, teaches natural and moral philosophy, unraveling the secrets of logic and revealing the hidden virtues of herbs and plants. His knowledge is vast and his power immense.

Buer is said to possess a particularly terrifying gift. He has the ability to cure all diseases, even the most lacerating, especially those affecting humans. But this benefit comes with a harrowing price: it is rumored that in order to heal a sick loved one, Buer requires the soul of the one who calls upon him. A dark pact where desperation intertwines with the ambition to obtain the power of healing. According to the disturbing "Book of Saint Cyprian," Buer is subjugated by the demon Agaliareth, a hint that even in the depths of hell, dark hierarchies and alliances rule the lives of these demonic entities.

BUER'S SEAL

Budú, also known as Vudú, Vodú, and Voodoo: An African god of witchcraft, depicted as a giant idol on the island of Ceylon. He taught the art that bears his name to the great sorcerers of the Ceylon tribes.

Chaigidiei: A Kabbalistic archdemon who opposes the influence of God himself.

Chamgaz: Among the veiled mysteries of Hebrew mythology, Chamgaz emerges as a demon of the shadows, though his presence remains shrouded in the darkness of demonic lore.

Chamuco, also known as Quigen and Kuijen: A mock demonic reference inspired by non-Catholic evangelical Christian churches. In America, he is seen as a representation of Satan.

Cheitan: A demon born from smoke.

Chiridirilles: A protective demon of travelers, appearing as a black man riding a horse.

Chu-Chiang: The infernal god of Chinese Taoism; he presides over the Second Hall of Horrors.

Cieguecillo: A small devil who resides in fire as his natural element, often identified with the salamander. He was born from a spark that flew from Vulcan's forge into the heart of Preneste.

Cimejes: An infernal Marquis. He is a mighty warrior who rides a black horse, with the power to locate lost or hidden treasures, to teach the trivium, and to transform a man into a warrior in his own likeness.

Cocytus: A Greek infernal river-demon. The Cocytus, with its murky waters, was formed from the tears of the damned souls.

Coep: A demonic reference to the crossbreed of various living beings. It is depicted with the head of a wild animal like a wolf, a human torso, and large black legs (including a jaguar-like tail). Coep is a leading figure among Latin demons.

Dahaka: A Persian demon of death, deceit, and lies; described with three heads, his body is covered in scorpions and lizards.

Dantalian, also known as Dantalion: An infernal Duke depicted as a man with multiple faces (both male and female), holding a book in his right hand. He teaches Arts and Sciences and has the power to influence the thoughts of men, turning good into evil.

Decarabia: A demon mentioned in demonology and in the dark arts of summoning, he holds a place within the sinister ranks of the Pseudomonarchia Daemonum and The Lesser Key of Solomon. He appears in the sixty-ninth position as a Marquis of Hell. However, in the Pseudomonarchia Daemonum, he is listed at the fifty-second spot without mentioning his title.

His form resembles a five-pointed star, which he can transform at will when invoked, assuming a more human appearance. Decarabia commands thirty legions of demons and holds dominion over birds. His knowledge encompasses the virtues of plants and precious stones, making him a being with hidden secrets.

However, one of his most notable powers is the ability to transform the caster into a winged creature, be it a bird or a bat. This aspect of his ability makes him both intriguing and terrifying, adding to his aura of mystery. It has been suggested that his name bears similarity to the word "Abracadabra", leading to speculation that Decarabia could be a demonic reinterpretation of the ancient Egyptian and Gnostic god, Abraxas. However, his true nature and origin remain an enigma in the depths of demonology.

STAMP OF DECARABIA

Demogorgon: The enigmatic genius of the earth emerges as a gaunt old man, draped in moss, dwelling in the very core of the planet. His rough and grimy figure shines with the wisdom of a seasoned sorcerer, capable of commanding ghosts and spirits of the air with his formidable will. In mythology, this being becomes synonymous with the Greek demon, an entity that lurks in the shadows, unknown and mysterious to humankind.

Drugia, also known as Druj, Drug, and Drauga: She is a creature of darkness, a formidable lieutenant of Ahriman, the dark lord known as "the Plague." Her touch, subtler than the shadow itself, unleashes both known and unknown diseases, embodying a demonic form of femininity. Three heads, three mouths, six eyes, and a thousand senses adorn her being, revealing the complexity and mystery that surround her in a macabre dance.

Dumah: The angel of silence and death according to the Kabbalah, stands as the undisputed commander of the demons lurking in Gehenna. His presence imposes a sepulchral silence, and his influence extends to the darkest corners of existence, where death becomes a subtle echo of his command.

Éacus, also known as Aiacos: Stands as a prominent figure in Greek mythology, revered and feared as one of the three principal judges of the underworld. Alongside Minos and Rhadamanthys, Éacus presides over the eternal court of Hades, where the fates of souls are decided with unwavering authority. His domain specifically encompasses the judgment of Europeans, reflecting his earthly origin as the legendary king of the island of Aegina. In life, Éacus was known for his unparalleled sense of justice and piety, virtues so profound that the gods entrusted him with the solemn task of adjudicating the dead.

Eligos, also known as Abigor and Eligor: In the infernal realms, Eligos, also known as Abigor or Eligor, stands as a grand duke of hell, ruling over sixty legions of demons. Gifted with occult knowledge and the ability to glimpse the future, his gaze penetrates battlefields and the souls of warriors. His presence attracts favors from lords, knights, and other prominent figures of importance. Depictions of Eligos reveal an imposing figure, a knight armed with lance, banner, and scepter, the latter sometimes depicted as a serpent, as noted by some authors. In other visions, he manifests as an ethereal spectre, sometimes mounted on a winged horse, his dark, imposing aura instilling fear and respect in equal measure. His presence evokes the uncertainty and sinister might that only the most powerful demons can manifest in the realms beyond.

ELIGOS ILLUSTRATION

76

SAIL OF ELIGOS

Emma-Ō, also known as Yemma Ten, Yemma Dai O and Emma: She stands as the supreme monarch of hell in the rich cosmology of Japanese Buddhism. Her mission transcends the limits of the earthly, being the implacable judge of damned souls, charged with dictating the punishment they deserve for their sins in life. Her face, framed by a subtle malevolence, takes on red hues while she exhibits sharp fangs that serve as silent witnesses to the infernal justice she administers.

Empusa: A demon of fascinating nature, she chooses to always manifest herself at midday, weaving her cloak of mystery in the light of day. Described as a beautiful young woman, her left foot takes on the solidity of bronze, or sometimes reveals itself in the form of a donkey's hoof. In the lands of Russia, her footsteps echoed in the harvests, where, under the guise of a seductive widow, she broke the limbs of the reapers with charming cruelty. Legend places her as the direct envoy of Hecate, the goddess of witchcraft and magic, endowing her with a frightening figure that inspires fear and awe in equal measure. In her dance between beauty and horror, Empusa weaves an irresistible spell, seducing mortals with her presence as she executes her dark designs.

Erlik, also known as Erlik-Khan: Stands as the malevolent spirit ruling over the icy realms of Siberia, emerging as the Turkic-Mongolian god of the dead. In the shadowy depths of mythology, his presence is woven from the very fabric of darkness and death, taking on forms that challenge human understanding.

This sinister being sometimes appears with the head of a majestic bull, asserting his dominance with the sheer power and ferocity of the creature. Other depictions show him riding atop a bull, symbolizing his leadership on the journey to the underworld. In certain visions, his face transforms into the fierce visage of a buffalo, with horns encircled by flames, casting an infernal glow.

In his most terrifying form, Erlik bears two heads and four hands, wearing a necklace of skulls as a trophy of his conquests in the realm of the dead. In his right hand, he wields a scepter topped with a skull, a symbol of his authority over final destinies, while his left hand grasps a sharp sword, ready to defend his kingdom against any challenge.

Despite his position as the god of the dead, Erlik does not command reverential respect; rather, he is met with distrust and fear by those who seek to appease his wrath. Sacrifices of black animals are offered in a desperate attempt to quell the fury of this dark god who reigns over the frozen lands of Siberia. Amidst the smoke of sacrifices and the shadows of his dominion, Erlik-Khan remains an enigmatic and terrifying figure, stirring both intrigue and fear in equal measure.

Exael: The tenth angel, emerges as the master of dark arts, teaching humanity the craft of forging weapons and instruments of war. His knowledge, though laced with peril, grants mortals the power of destruction and conquest, revealing a duality between celestial light and the shadows of conflict.

Fecor: One of the three demons assigned as custodians of hidden treasures, Fecor stands as an unyielding guardian of riches beyond mortal sight. His subtle presence shrouds these treasures in a veil of mystery, challenging those who dare to seek the hidden wealth nestled in the darkest corners of the underworld.

Filotano: Also known as Philotanus, he is a second-tier demon and the loyal lieutenant of Belial. His influence spreads through the shadows of seduction, using sodomy and pederasty as tools to corrupt souls. Unlike his master, Philotanus does not partake directly in these acts but rather incites them from the shadows. His affinity for witchcraft makes him a protector of sorcerers, offering them his shelter against those who seek to unravel the secrets of the occult.

Flegazón: A powerful demon who bears the title of the chief of the Central Realm, Flegazón stands as a fearsome and dominant entity in the infernal hierarchies. His name echoes like the wind blowing through flames, and his reign at the very center of darkness adds an extra layer of terror to his presence. Amidst the flames and shadows, Flegazón leads with an iron hand, unleashing his power in the heart of the demonic realm.

Fleuretty: According to Christian literary teachings, Fleuretty emerges as the lieutenant general of Beelzebub, extending his dominion over the African lands. His expertise is intricately tied to plants considered "poisonous" from a psychotropic perspective, weaving a web of intrigue and seduction through nature's hidden secrets. This nocturnal demon, skilled in the arts of manipulation, not only stirs sexual desires in the dark but also sows the seeds of conflict and wars among men, acting as a mastermind of discord that dances in the shadows.

Florón: On the other hand, Florón is revealed as a familiar demon belonging to the order of the condemned Cherubim. In his fallen state, this dark being exerts his influence among the ranks of the fallen angels, carrying the curse of disobedience. His presence, marked by the paradox of beauty and damnation, stirs the waters of the infernal hierarchies, embodying the tragedy of those who once stood close to divinity and now slip into eternal shadows. Among whispers and sighs, Florón rises as a figure that encapsulates the inescapable duality of his fallen nature.

Focalor: The Grand Duke of Hell, Focalor, emerges with an imposing presence, commanding a legion of spirits, though the exact numbers vary across different demonological traditions. In the records of "The Lesser Key of Solomon," he is listed as the 41st of the 72 demons, inscribed within the dark pentacle of invocation. Focalor's appearance is that of a winged being with griffin-like features, blending the majesty of birds with the ferocity of mythological beasts. Focalor's power manifests itself with an uncontrollable fury, capable of drowning men and bringing down warships with an ease that only a storm lord could possess.

However, under the yoke of a skilled conjurer, this demon can be subdued and controlled, thus preventing it from causing unnecessary havoc. Its dominion extends over the wind and the sea, unleashing tremors on the land as easily as it conjures storms in the deepest waters.

Legend whispers that Focalor, in his former glory, harbored hopes of returning to heaven after a thousand years, but such hopes were betrayed by the darkness that envelops him. An intriguing connection is revealed by exploring the mysteries of demonology: Luciphagous Rofacale, one of the three archdemons, bears an anagram of Focalor's own name. This enigma suggests a deep and mysterious connection between these infernal beings, a bond that weaves itself into the deepest shadows of the underworld.

ILLUSTRATION AND SEAL OF
FOCALOR

Furfur: A Great Earl of Hell, he rules with iron authority over twenty-nine legions of demons. His appearance is intriguing and diverse, sometimes manifesting as a stag or a winged deer with human limbs and a flaming tail, while at other times, he takes the form of an angel, confusing the perception of those who behold him. This demon possesses a singular and dual power. On one hand, he is capable of engendering passionate love between a man and a woman, which can lead to obsession and madness. On the other, Furfur can summon unbridled elements of nature, causing storms, tempests, thunder, lightning, and hurricane-force winds.

At his core, Furfur is a being prone to lying, unless he is forced into a magical triangle, where he is forced to answer truthfully. In this way, he reveals secrets of both the occult and divine worlds, and can even address the most abstract questions, albeit in a harsh, dissonant voice.

FURFUR

The meaning behind the name "Furfur" is enigmatic. In Latin, "Furfur" can be translated as "bran" or "bran." Some argue that its name is a variant of "Furcifer," meaning "scoundrel," "rogue," or "scoundrel."

The duality in Furfur's name seems to mirror the ambivalent nature of this demon. In the realm of occultism and tarot, intriguing connections have been established. According to Travis McHenry's Occult Tarot, Furfur is associated with the Ten of Cups, further deepening his enigmatic nature in the esoteric sphere.

Furcas: The infernal knight of profound knowledge, Furcas stands out as a master of the arcane arts and dark philosophy. This cruel, ancient being imparts his wisdom in disciplines such as pyromancy, palmistry, logic, rhetoric, astronomy, and philosophy. He is depicted as an elderly figure with a long beard and hair, riding through the vastness of the underworld on a shadowy steed.

Gadrel: In the higher echelons of Hebrew mythology, Gadrel rises as a demon of formidable rank. His presence, shrouded in an aura of mystery, exudes authority and a dark majesty. Within the corridors of the inferno, Gadrel stands as an undisputed lord of shadows, weaving his influence into the very fabric of eternity. Gamaliel: Revealed as a Kabbalistic archdemon, Gamaliel is an entity that fosters obscenity and perversion in the depths of occultism. His presence acts as a shroud that taints purity, luring mortals into indulging in forbidden pleasures and paths of decadence. In the delicate dance between light and shadow, Gamaliel rises as an architect of depravity, guiding those who seek the darkest secrets of existence.

Gamchicoth: A Kabbalistic archdemon who ensnares and entangles all things, weaving confusion and disorder throughout the spiritual and material realms.

Gaziel, also known as Goziel: He stands as the demon guardian of hidden treasures buried deep underground. This cunning entity, who delights in the play of shadows, possesses the skill to relocate treasures just as they are about to be discovered, leaving behind the eerie echo of ghostly bell chimes that shroud daring seekers in a mantle of terror. His most intriguing ability lies in his power to resurrect the dead, a dark force that stirs within the deepest shadows.

Gaziel shares his existence with a companion entity known as Almudena, a force embodying deception and fantasy, weaving illusions into the very fabric of reality. This demon, whose reign is founded on illusion, acts as the king in the court of lies, ensnaring those who venture into realms of deceit and imagination.

It is said that Gaziel can transform into a dog, a form that some believe to be his original essence. This metamorphosis adds an extra layer of mystery and awe to the legend of Gaziel, a being who navigates through the shadows with the skill of a thief of secrets and hidden treasures.

Gila: The infamous witch of the 16th century emerges from the annals of history as a fearsome figure. Her insatiable appetite for human flesh, especially that of children, has immortalized her in dark legends still whispered among wet nurses. One tale recounts her attempt to devour the young Emperor Maurice, but her malevolent efforts were thwarted by the protective talismans he carried. Despite the centuries that have passed, Gila's name remains a specter on the lips of those who respect and fear the forces of darkness.

Goab (or Goap): The sovereign of Hell's western region, Goab commands the demons of the midday, guiding shadows with his infernal mantle. This king of darkness responds to invocations from 3:00 AM to noon and again from 9:00 PM until midnight. During these specific times, the forces under his rule awaken, ready to obey his commands in the underworld.

Gob: Gob emerges as a demon deeply rooted in the very essence of the earth. His influence reaches the subterranean depths, where he triggers sinkholes, seismic movements, and the release of asphyxiating and deadly gases. This dark entity imbues poisonous substances with lethal properties and presides over the spread of plagues and epidemics. Gob intervenes in human misfortunes, stirring the darkest passions of greed, pride, and cruelty. His true obsession, avarice, drives him to stoke human greed, leading hearts down dark and tortuous paths. The figure of Gob serves as a reminder of the forces lurking deep within the earth and shadows, intertwining his power with tragic events and human suffering. In the silence of darkness, Gob stands as a sinister entity, a weaver of fates and master of dark arts that dance in the twilight of existence.

Golab: The Kabbalistic archdemon Golab is known as the instigator of the consuming fires that sweep across the earth. He embodies the raw, destructive force of uncontained flames, igniting chaos wherever he treads. His presence is felt in the shadows, a harbinger of devastation that lurks in the unseen corners of the world. When Golab stirs, the very air thickens with the scent of burning ash, and the ground trembles as if anticipating the inferno to come.

This fiery and sinister entity emerges from the darkness with a malevolent grin, his form flickering like the flames he commands.

Goleo Binban (or Beenban): Known as the demon of the desert, Goleo Binban emerges as the spirit lurking among the dunes and shadows of the barren wasteland. His influence preys upon the melancholic, piercing their souls with the deepest loneliness. Referred to as the "spirit of solitude," Goleo Binban glides across the desert sands, woven into the fabric of silence and melancholy that envelops those who wander the vast and desolate expanse.

Gresil: The demon of impurity, Gresil embodies the essence of corruption in its darkest form. This malevolent being manifests in the absence of purity and moral decay, steering hearts and minds towards the paths of depravity. In his subtle dance, Gresil becomes the very personification of impurity, weaving his influence into the darkest corners of existence. In a world where purity is cherished, Gresil's presence serves as a constant reminder of the shadows lurking within the human soul.

Guayota: A demonic figure from Guanche mythology, Guayota makes his dwelling deep within the majestic Teide, the towering mountain of Tenerife, Spain. In the shadows of this volcanic peak, Guayota embodies darkness and mystery, intricately woven into the legends whispered among the mists of Guanche lore. His influence extends to the mountain's most hidden crevices, where shadows dance with subterranean flames, fueling both fear and reverence for this ancient demon.

Guta: The Hungarian demon Guta reveals itself as an entity that strikes its victims down to death. This figure of cruelty and violence is entrenched in the legends that have endured through time, a menacing presence that emanates an aura of relentless brutality.

Haagenti: A sinister president of the infernal pits, Haagenti emerges in demonic mythology as a monstrous figure that strikes terror into all who behold him. His appearance takes two terrifying forms: as a fearsome dragon or as a winged bull with griffin-like features, adding an aura of evil to his image. In the infernal court, Haagenti stands as an undisputed ruler, unleashing his power in the shadows and carrying with him the very essence of terror that emanates from the demonic depths. His name resonates like an ominous echo in the halls of the underworld, reminding mortals of the dark majesty of this infernal president.

This demon, despite his malignancy, possesses deep and disturbing knowledge. Under his teachings, mortals can acquire wisdom, but this wisdom is tinged with dark purposes. Haagenti reveals the most hermetic secrets, such as the transmutation of water into wine and vice versa, or the alchemy that turns metals into gold. However, these lessons do not seek good or enlightenment, but lead to perversion, debauchery and crime. Haagenti personifies the darkest and most seductive side of forbidden knowledge, attracting those who seek power and riches without scruples.

Habondia: A demon of the highest rank, Habondia is known as the demon king of the fairies, ruling over these mystical creatures with a power that transcends the boundaries of reality and the magical realms. In the shadows of the underworld, Habondia exerts his influence over the faerie kingdom, orchestrating the dance of the fairies in harmony with the dark secrets hidden within his very essence.

Häel: A powerful and influential devil in the depths of Hell, Häel stands as a figure of unparalleled authority within the infernal hierarchies. His influence stretches across the vast abyss, serving as the supreme leader upon whom countless dark spirits depend. Häel's presence reverberates through the darkness, marking his domain with a sinister majesty and an unyielding command.

Hallulaya: An ancient Babylonian demon of the old shadows, Hallulaya reveals himself as a tormentor of men along their journeys. His presence lurks at crossroads and along lonely paths, bringing anguish to those who venture into the uncertainty of travel. In Babylonian mythology, Hallulaya embodies a creeping shadow, sowing unease and fear in the hearts of mortals who traverse the winding roads.

Harab Serap: A Kabbalistic archdemon, Harab Serap is known as the bringer of failures in the dark cosmology of the occult arts. His influence weaves through the threads of misfortune and defeat, unleashing his power to sow chaos in the paths of those who dare to challenge the infernal forces. Amidst failures and laments, Harab Serap stands as a figure embodying the shadows that cloud success and fortune.

Herodias: Also known as Noctiluca, she emerges as the Queen of the Night, presiding over the sabbats and demanding human sacrifices.

Her cult thrived during the 12th century, with her sinister figure deeply intertwined with the mysterious rituals performed under the cloak of darkness. In the dim light of the sabbats, the presence of Herodias instilled both fear and devotion, revealing herself as a powerful entity who exerted her influence over the darkest corners of worship and arcane practices.

Hiranya Kaśipu ('golden bed') and Hiranyāksha ('golden eyes'): In Hindu mythology, these demonic brothers take human form and terrorize the realms with their tyranny. To end their reign of terror, the god Vishnu incarnated twice—first as Varāha, the mighty boar, and later as Narasinha, a fearsome half-man, half-lion being. These divine avatars served as instruments of justice, bringing about the destruction of the wicked brothers. Their battles epitomize the eternal struggle between good and evil, a central theme in Hindu mythology.

Humtaba: A demon of Babylonian origin, Humtaba is depicted as a terrifying entity with a flame-spewing mouth and a deadly breath. His fearsome presence looms large in the legends of ancient Babylon, where he embodies the lurking terror of the shadows, striking fear into the hearts of those who encounter his relentless ferocity.

Hades: The Greek god of the underworld and ruler of the dead, Hades stands as a formidable figure in Greek mythology. Overseeing the realm of the deceased, he commands authority in the depths of the underworld, where the souls of the departed find their eternal resting place. Shrouded in darkness and solemnity, Hades personifies the unavoidable transition from life to death, embodying the somber inevitability of the human condition.

IIblis (Iblis al-Quadim, Eblis, Al-Harith, Azail, Sheitán, Satan): In Islamic tradition, Iblis is an archdemon and the supreme leader of the demonic djinn. He is often associated with the peacock, drawing a symbolic connection to the deity Melek Tawus. Iblis is typically depicted as a foolish spirit adorned with peacock feathers and bearing the head of a mule. He is portrayed as androgynous, possessing a sexual organ on each leg, allowing him to self-fertilize. As a result, Iblis lays ten eggs daily, each hatching into either 70 male demons (shaytān) or female demons (shaytāna). Everything around him is venomous. The name "Iblis" is thought to be a phonetic adaptation of the Greek word "diábolos," meaning "to flow downward."

Isabô: A demonic entity of infernal nature, Isabô is depicted with expansive wings and powerful fists. This mysterious figure, steeped in dark allure, is a captivating presence for those who delve into the hidden corners of spirituality. With wings unfurled and fists clenched, Isabô exudes an ancient and enigmatic energy, drawing the curious deeper into the realms of the unknown.

Ishtar, Isthar, Zarpanith, Belit, Attar, Sarpanit, Astarte, Terpanit, Milita, and Ashtar: Known as the enigmatic Chaldean goddess, Ishtar was venerated across the regions of Babylon and Assyria. She was the embodiment of fertility rituals and presided over domains as diverse as beauty, love, war, victory, and other essential aspects of life. However, Ishtar's legacy took a darker turn in later ages. As successive religions emerged, they began to view her with suspicion, leading to her demonization. Despite her origins as a goddess of fertility and a revered figure of vital life aspects, the passage of time and the evolution of religious beliefs shrouded her in mystery and contradiction, transforming her from a celebrated deity into a figure cloaked in shadows and myth.

Ipos: The enigmatic Earl of the Infernal Pits, he exudes an aura of mystery and power in the realm of demonology. With authority over thirty-six legions of demons, he is among the most influential entities in the underworld. His knowledge encompasses the secrets of the past, present, and future, granting him a supernatural insight that few can match. Some accounts suggest that Ipos can instill wit and courage in men, elevating them above their mortal condition. Ipos' depiction is as strange as his nature, adding a touch of eerie uniqueness to his figure. He is described as a hybrid creature: an angelic body, the head of a lion, the tail of a hare, and the feet of a goose. However, he occasionally manifests with a leonine body, and on rare occasions, he assumes the form of a vulture. These metamorphoses underscore his ability to adapt and change, further confusing those who venture to evoke him.

With its arcane equivalent to the 2 of Wands in the Tarot, it spans a zodiacal decan that extends from March 22 to 31, suggesting a connection with spring, renewal and duality. Its presence stands as a reminder that wisdom and knowledge can be as ambiguous as the creatures that represent it.

IPOS SEAL

TPOS ILLUSTRATION

Ivannus: A being of the shadows, raised to the heights of the underworld, his form extends to an imposing height, with long, wide horns adorned with two pentagram inscriptions on his back. In occult circles and in the corners of European tradition, he is popularly known as Ivann.

Jana: Being of outstanding power, prominent member among the Divi Spirits, along with Saracil, Sathiel and Amon, among other dark beings.

Junier: Demon of indomitable power, prince of the angelic shadows that bow before his presence.

Kelby or Kelpy: A malevolent water spirit that takes the form of a dark horse, Kelby is an ominous figure sometimes seen holding a torch burning with the flames of damnation.

Kellen, or Kelen: The Ruler of Forbidden Loves. Alongside his companion Nisroc, Kellen governs over illicit romances, debauchery, and orgies. A seductive entity, he exploits the weaknesses of the human heart to weave bonds in the darkness. In his domain, Kellen's whispers stir the deepest excesses and awaken forbidden passions, drawing souls into the abyss of sinful desires.

Kerobal, or Turban Querobal: The Turkish Spell. Kerobal, also known as Turban Querobal, is a demon of Turkish origin, invoked by witches in malevolent rituals. Called upon in times of need, he unleashes curses and enchantments charged with dark energy. The shadows surrounding Kerobal reveal his deep ties to black magic and the hidden secrets of witchcraft practices.

Kisín: The Advocate of Ah-puch. Linked to Ah-puch, the Mayan god of death, Kisín manifests as a skeletal and terrifying figure. This entity, akin to the Semitic concept of Satan, embodies the inevitability of death and decay. His presence invokes both fear and reverence, serving as a stark reminder of life's fleeting nature.

Kobal, Kabal, and Robals: The Treacherous Theatrical Director of Hell. Kobal, also known as Kabal and Robals, takes on the role of the general director in the infernal theaters of the underworld. The patron of demonic comedians, his wicked laughter echoes through sinister performances. Yet behind the facade of amusement, Kobal is a cunning demon who bites and harms with deceit, exposing the dark side of infernal comedy and the biting irony within his tragic plays.

Kumbhákarna: The Ceylonese Colossus of Interrupted Slumber In the narratives of Hindu mythology, Kumbhákarna is a fearsome giant whose name translates to 'ears like pots.' Described as a colossal Ceylonese monster towering up to 420 kilometers tall, Kumbhákarna's legend is immortalized in Chapter 6 of the Rāmāyana. He would awaken only one day every six months, and during his brief period of wakefulness, his formidable presence cast a shadow of terror and challenge across the land. However, his reign of intermittent dreams was ultimately cut short by the god Rāma, who brought an end to his daunting existence.

Labasú: The Harbinger of Misfortune, whose name means 'the one who topples,' emerges from the depths of Babylonian mythology as a demon who embodies the burden of misfortune. This detestable figure was seen as a malevolent thief, bringing calamity to every household he haunted. Labasú looms as an ominous entity, lurking in the shadows, evading the light of prosperity, and casting a pall of despair wherever he appears.

Lagasse: The Demon of Hypocrisy In the chronicles of the occult, Lagasse is revealed as the demon of hypocrisy. This sinister entity revels in duplicity and deceit, cloaking its true nature beneath a guise of sincerity while weaving intricate webs of lies and betrayal. Lagasse personifies the shadow that hides behind appearances, reminding us of the fragility of truth and how easily hypocrisy can take root in the darkest corners of the human heart.

Lamashtu, Lamastu, and Labartu: The Dark Assyro-Babylonian DeityLamashtu, also known as Lamastu and Labartu, rises from the shadows of Assyro-Babylonian mythology as a malevolent deity, the daughter of Anu. This fearsome female demon is depicted in a terrifying form:

A woman's torso with the head and claws of a lion, donkey-like ears and teeth, outstretched wings, and a chilling pose as she nurses two wolf cubs while seated on a donkey. Her essence is dark, barren, and insatiable, embodying a primal, destructive force that preys upon the vulnerable and weak.

Lamashtu: The Terror of Childbirth, Lamashtu instills deep fear, particularly among women in labor and nursing mothers, who dread her potential to harm newborns. This malevolent entity possesses the ability to take on seven different forms, marking her as one of the seven dark forces that haunt ancient Babylon. Her presence serves as a chilling reminder of life's fragility and the ongoing struggle against the malevolent powers lurking in the shadows.

Lanithro: The Demon of the Air, Lanithro stands as the demon of the air, a being that moves through the invisible currents enveloping the world. His essence is intertwined with the atmosphere, and his presence can be felt in the winds that whisper dark secrets. As the master of the elements in the realm of the occult, Lanithro embodies the untamed forces of nature itself, manifesting in bursts of mystery and aerial power.

Leraje: The Infernal Marquis of Conflict, also known as Leraie, Leraikha, Leraye, Loray, and Oray, Leraje is a grand infernal marquis who incites great battles and disputes. He is portrayed as a strikingly handsome archer dressed in green, armed with a bow. Leraje's presence heralds the onset of conflict, as he revels in sowing discord and chaos through his uncanny archery skills.

Leshy: The Slavic Forest Demon Leshy, born from the union of a devil and a human woman, is a Slavic demon resembling a human but with the legs, ears, and horns of a goat, much like a Greek satyr.

Lethe: The Greek River DemonLethe is the infernal river of Greek mythology, whose waters possess the power to make those who drink from it forget their past entirely. This demon-river embodies the concept of oblivion, offering a respite from the burdens of memory at the cost of one's identity, leaving behind an existence shrouded in amnesia.

Leviathan: The Primordial Serpent of Chaos, In Judaism, Ugaritic mythology introduces us to Lotan, a multi-headed, serpent-like monster embodying primordial chaos, heralding the beginning of Creation. Psalm 74 alludes to this being, emphasizing its role as a powerful entity tied to the forces of disorder. In the Book of Job, there is mention of magicians who could supposedly resurrect Leviathan, but it is prophesied that God will ultimately destroy it at the end of times. However, the most detailed depiction of Leviathan can be found in Job 41.

In Genesis, Leviathan is implicitly referenced as a serpent, hinted at through the phrase "God created the great sea monsters," suggesting its lurking presence. The medieval Jewish scholar Rashi interpreted this as a reappearance of the serpent that tempted Adam and Eve in the Garden of Eden. According to legend, God initially created both a male and female Leviathan but later sacrificed the female, reserving her as a feast for the righteous. This was done to prevent the Leviathans from reproducing, as their offspring could threaten the existence of the world. The term "Taninim" in this context can be translated as "sea monster, crocodile, or great serpent," highlighting the colossal and terrifying nature of these mythological creatures.

In Christian tradition, Leviathan is often seen as a demonic entity, frequently associated with Satan or the Devil.

Some interpretations even speculate that Leviathan and Rahab are the same creature (Isaiah 51:9), a connection drawn from biblical references depicting Leviathan as a malevolent force, an adversary of God. In "Enuma Elish," the storm god Marduk slays Tiamat, a seven-headed sea monster and goddess of Chaos and Creation, and creates the earth and heaven from the two halves of Tiamat's body.

In this context, some biblical scholars view Leviathan as representing the forces of chaos and evil, and its defeat by God symbolizes victory over chaos and the establishment of divine order in the world. Leviathan thus becomes a symbol of the struggle between good and evil, and its connection to Satan in Christian tradition reinforces this demonic association in religious interpretation.

LEVIATHAN

Licas, also known as Lycas and Alybas: The Demon of the Thames Licas, a dark entity from England, is known as the Demon of the Thames. This creature was described as pitch black, with a foul-smelling body covered in wolf's hide. In ancient times, annual human sacrifices were offered to appease this fearsome being, an eerie ritual that marked his influence over the river's murky waters.

Lilitu, also known as Lilit and Lilith: The First Woman and Demoness Lilith is a mysterious figure rooted in Mesopotamian mythology, known as the first woman created before Eve. Her name is steeped in legend, representing a powerful feminine demon who holds the rank of a Principality in the demonic hierarchy. Lilith is said to lead the succubi, female demons who seduce men, draining their vital essence and igniting the spark of life that births other demons.

This dark entity, shrouded in lust and forbidden desire, feeds off acts of lechery and erotic dreams, leaving men weakened in a whirlwind of impurity. Every carnal encounter steeped in depravity serves as a tribute to this deity of lust, weaving a web of sin and mystery under the cover of night. A demonic presence cloaked in allure and unease, Lilith lurks in the shadows, a harbinger of temptation and peril.

Mesopotamian Origins: In ancient Mesopotamian religions, Lilith was regarded as a female spirit or demon linked to storms and chaos. She was believed to bring misfortune, illness, and death. Her earliest known mention dates back to around 3000 BCE in Sumerian religion, where she was called "Lilitu." As a figure of disruption, she embodied the unpredictable and destructive forces of nature, feared for the calamities she was said to unleash.

In Jewish Tradition: from the 6th century CE onward, Lilith began to appear in rabbinic literature and Jewish magical incantation bowls. In medieval Jewish folklore, she evolved into a feared entity often depicted as the first wife of Adam, created before Eve. Unlike the obedient Eve, Lilith was portrayed as a rebellious and independent figure who refused to submit to Adam, leading to her expulsion from Eden. This myth set the stage for her transformation into a demoness, a symbol of untamed feminine power and seduction that haunted the imaginations of those who encountered her legend.

According to this version, Lilith refused to obey Adam, which led to her either running away or being banished from Eden. She preferred to live with the demons rather than return to Adam. This image has been used to symbolize independence and defiance of traditional femininity.

SEAL OF LILITH

Modern Development: The figure of Lilith has continued to develop in the 19th and 20th centuries. As women's emancipation progressed in the Western world, Lilith became a symbol of femininity that does not submit to the masculine. Her image has been linked to the Mother Goddess and female independence. Lilith remains a theme present in popular culture, literature, astrology, and the occult.

ILLUSTRATION
OF LILITH

Lilu, also known as Lilla: One of the three night demons in Mesopotamian mythology, alongside Lilit and Ardat Lili. Lilu is a wandering male spirit, rooted in Akkadian myth. He is akin to the figure of a vampire.

Lucifer: A word woven with threads of light and darkness, emerging as the bearer of radiance in the vast expanse of the heavens. This term is shrouded in mystery, born in an era when humanity gazed at the sky, awestruck by the enigma veiling the brilliance of the planet Venus.

In ancient times, Venus, with its radiant glow at dawn, baffled early observers, blurring the line between star and planet. As the "morning star," it seemed to vie with the celestial lights around it, crafting a narrative that delves into its relationship with both dusk and dawn. Roman tradition distinguished between the "morning star" and the "evening star," further deepening the mystery surrounding Lucifer. In Christian mythology, this name became associated with the fallen angel, whose beauty and wisdom led to arrogance, transforming him into Satan himself. A biblical passage, Isaiah 14:12, references "Helel ben Shachar," the "shining one, son of the morning," translated as "Lucifer" in the Vulgate. Thus, Lucifer stands as the embodiment of both fall and rebellion, a figure poised at the boundary between light and shadow.

Throughout history, the name "Lucifer" has oscillated between glorification and demonization. His story is steeped in dualities: light and darkness, good and evil. In Christian tradition, he is the archetype of the fallen angel, the bringer of light who became the prince of darkness.

This duality suggests that the line between the divine and the demonic is blurred and fragile, reminding us that beauty and power can lead to ruin. However, despite this dark portrayal, Lucifer has also been reimagined in popular culture as a symbol of rebellion, independence, and freedom. He is often depicted challenging divine authority, questioning imposed rules, and seeking enlightenment through knowledge. This aspect of Lucifer invites us to reflect on the nature of morality and free will.

Ultimately, the mystery surrounding Lucifer lies in his ability to embody both the fall and the rise, darkness and light, rebellion and liberation. He is a symbol that transcends mere duality, challenging our conventional notions of good and evil, inviting us to explore the complexities of the human condition and the eternal questioning of the divine.

LUCIFER

Lul: Considered a lower-order demon in Hebrew mythology, Lul manifests as an entity of shadows and subtlety. His presence evokes an unsettling sensation, often linked to minor misfortunes and disturbances in everyday life. Though he lacks the grandeur of some of his demonic counterparts, Lul is said to work insidiously in the dark corners of existence, influencing the small miseries of those who cross his path.

Magistelo: Magistelo, a demon inclined toward collaboration with practitioners of the dark arts, takes on seductive forms, appearing as either a succubus or an incubus. This cunning and manipulative being aligns with witches and warlocks in their quest for knowledge and power. Acting as a dark guide, Magistelo offers arcane secrets and mystical abilities in exchange for pacts and commitments. His presence often weaves a web of deceit and sensual pleasures, luring the unsuspecting into the whirlpool of black magic.

Malphas: A powerful Grand President of the dark underworld, Malphas commands forty legions of demons. He serves under Satan, holding the second rank in the infernal hierarchy. His abilities are as diverse as they are terrifying. Malphas is known for his skill in constructing houses, towering structures, and fortresses, as well as for his capacity to dismantle the works of his enemies. Moreover, he intrudes upon the thoughts and desires of others, revealing hidden and disturbing secrets to the bold magicians who dare to summon him.

Despite his malevolent nature, Malphas is also a provider of good familiar spirits. This dark figure possesses the power to call forth artisans from every corner of the world at the will of his invoker. However, interactions with this demon are fraught with peril.

Malphas' appearance is intriguing, initially manifesting as a raven, a creature that symbolizes darkness and mystery. But under certain circumstances or upon request, he can assume a human form with a raspy voice, a transition that adds an additional element of eeriness to his already dark nature.

The price of summoning Malphas is high, however, as this demon cannot be trusted. Despite his apparent cooperation, it is often said that he will deceive those who try to harness his power. His enigmatic and treacherous figure adds to the rich and terrifying lore of demonology, reminding us that dealings with dark beings rarely end without sinister consequences.

M
A
L
P
H
A
S

MALPHAS SEAL

Marbas: An enigmatic president of the infernal hosts, he appears before us in two notable forms. His most powerful image is that of a majestic lion, a ferocious beast that radiates an imposing presence. But when called upon by mortals in search of his wisdom and power, this demon takes the form of a human, hiding his terrifying nature. At his command, thirty-six legions of demons await his command, ready to do his bidding and reveal dark secrets.

Marbas is a being of duality, capable of both causing disease and granting healing. He can infuse mechanical knowledge and unique abilities into those who dare to call upon him. Making a deal with Marbas is no simple task, however. Those who desire his knowledge must be willing to wager their souls in exchange. Only one question will be answered, and only with the truth, at the cost of the summoner's own soul. The loss of this soul prevents future summonings while alive, unless the sorcerer is willing to offer more souls in sacrifice.

MARBAS

Magoa: A formidable entity of the Eastern shadows, Magoa is the monarch of a dark realm who, with his infernal wisdom, answers the questions posed by the bold seekers who dare to seek his counsel.

Mahonin: A lesser demon hailing from the depths of the third hierarchy and the second order of archangels; Mahonin's dwelling lies among mystical waters, woven with threads of enigma.

Mania, also known as Lalaria: An Etruscan deity of the underworld, Mania was an ancient divinity worshipped during the dark Compitalia festivals, alongside the Lares. She is considered the matron or grandmother of the Manes and the goddess of silence. In her rituals, offerings of poppies, dogs, and human sacrifices were made in her honor; her figure, both terrifying and sublime, would manifest in all its majesty.

Mantor: In the ancient Chaldean lands, Mantor stood as a demon embodying fever. His presence was like a shadow sliding through the darkness, bringing with it discomfort and weakness. As his breath touched mortals, illness took hold, turning health into a mere illusion.

Mantus: The Deformed Monarch of the Infernal Realms. In Etruscan myths, Mantus ruled the underworld with a grotesque and terrifying figure. Armed with a saber or a mace, his wings beat the air while his crown glowed with the majesty of the netherworld. Those who ventured into his presence faced the horrifying vision of a deity who reigned over eternal darkness.

Magoa: A formidable entity of Eastern shadows, Magoa stands as the sovereign of a dark realm, wielding infernal wisdom. He responds to the queries of those intrepid souls who dare to seek his counsel, guiding them through the murky paths of forbidden knowledge.

Mahonin: A lesser demon originating from the depths of the third hierarchy and the second order of archangels. Mahonin dwells in mystical waters, shrouded in threads of enigma, embodying the mysteries of the deep.

Mania, also known as Lalaria: An ancient Etruscan goddess of the underworld, Mania was venerated during the somber Compitalia festivals, in the company of the Lares. Revered as the matron or grandmother of the Manes and the goddess of silence, her rituals involved offerings of poppies, dogs, and even human sacrifices. Her presence was both terrifying and sublime, manifesting in all her majestic glory.

Mantor: In the ancient Chaldean lands, Mantor was a demon who personified fever. His dark presence swept like a shadow, bringing discomfort and weakness. As his breath touched the living, illness would take hold, transforming the once vibrant health of his victims into a mere illusion of well-being.

Mantus: The Deformed Monarch of the Infernal Realms. In Etruscan mythology, Mantus ruled over the underworld with a grotesque and fearsome visage. Armed with a saber or mace, his wings cut through the air, while his crown shone with the infernal brilliance of the netherworld. Those who dared to approach him faced a terrifying deity, the sovereign of eternal darkness.

The myth of Mephistopheles spread with Romanticism and was popularized by Faust, an iconic literary work. It embodies an existential conflict: the decline of faith and the rise of moral pragmatism in advanced societies. In this context, Mephistopheles becomes a symbol of the loss of faith and the adoption of a moral system of one's own.

MEPHISTOPHELES

This demon is often portrayed as a tragicomic character, caught between his success in undermining the supremacy of God in the minds of the masses and his own defeat in losing relevance due to the same process. He is depicted with great sophistication, dressed in sumptuous clothes befitting nobility. His cold, rational and logical mind becomes his main tool to seduce people and manipulate them into following his designs.

Megara: One of the three Greek Furies (Eumenides or Erinyes) of Tartarus.

Melanisalcayuto: This demon is a myth in the world of demons, he is very powerful.

Melek Tawus, The Splendor of the Peacock Angel: In the mystical rituals of the Yazidi religion, Melek Tawus, also known as Melek Ta'ûs, emerges as a celestial figure of singular splendor. His name, literally translated as "Peacock Angel," reflects his connection to the majesty of this winged creature. Though some may label him a Mesopotamian demon, for the Yazidis, Melek Tawus is much more; he is the supreme leader of the archangels. His form is an intriguing amalgamation, appearing as a peacock, a rooster, or even a hybrid that fuses the essence of both creatures into a divine being.

Merigaz: In the shadows of Hebrew mythology, Merigaz manifests as a lesser demon, whispering his presence in the darkest corners. His subtle nature intertwines with mystical narratives, where his influence extends into the twilight of the unknown.

Merihim: Prince of pestilence and master of the infernal air, Merihim is the supreme ruler of the winds and the leader of demons who bring plague and disease. His presence glides through the currents of malevolent winds, carrying a dark curse that befalls those under his influence. In the infernal realm, Merihim commands the poisoned breezes and leads his legions of demons, spreading misery and desolation in his wake.

Minos: Among the three judges of the Greek underworld, Minos holds a prominent position. His role is to judge those whose fates Aeacus and Rhadamanthus could not determine. With unwavering wisdom, Minos evaluates the deeds of the deceased, assigning their destinies in the vast realm of the dead.

Minosón, Succubus of Trickery entrusted to Häel: Her nefarious mission is to weave invisible threads into the vast tapestry of games of chance, guaranteeing victory in all its forms. Under the aegis of Häel, Minosón delights in influencing the passions and ambitions of those who venture into the world of games, where her subtle presence propels players toward triumph, in a pact that carries with it an unknown price.

Morax: Known also as Marax or Foraii in demonology, he holds a prominent position as the Great Earl and President of Hell. Under his command, he is said to control a legion consisting of thirty-six demons, although some authors claim the number is thirty-two. His knowledge spans fields such as astronomy and other liberal sciences. Additionally, he has the power to bestow wise and benevolent familiar spirits who possess a deep understanding of the virtues of herbs and precious stones. Morax's visual representation shows him as an imposing bull with the face of a man. His name appears to be derived from the Latin term "morax," which suggests delay or delay, although his role in demonology focuses more on knowledge and connection to the spirit world than delay.

MORAX

Moloch: Although not a demon in the traditional sense of demonology, like the demons often depicted in popular religions and beliefs, Moloch is a figure that appears in certain ancient texts, particularly the Bible, as a pagan deity worshipped by some peoples in ancient times. In the Bible, specifically the Old Testament, Moloch is mentioned as a deity to whom child sacrifices were offered.

The worship of Moloch involved the heinous practice of burning children alive as offerings. References to this are found in books such as Leviticus and Jeremiah. Although Moloch is not considered a demon in the classical demonological sense, his name has often been associated with evil and cruelty due to the sacrificial practices attributed to him in the Bible. The figure of Moloch has been the subject of theological and literary interpretation throughout history and has influenced the representation of evil in various cultural works.

MOLOCH

Morail: Among the shadows of the supernatural, Morail emerges as a demon with a peculiar gift: the power to render any being invisible. His craft unfolds in mystery, shrouding those under his influence in the veil of the unseen. In the dance of the hidden, Morail stands as a master manipulator of reality, weaving his magic to cloak individuals from prying eyes.

Munkir, also known as Munchir: In Muslim narratives, Munkir, also referred to as Munchir, appears as a dark angel of malevolent nature. Alongside his companion Nékir, they dwell in Adhab Algab, the Islamic purgatory, where they torment the wicked. With their ominous presence, these black angels become the enforcers of punishment, unleashing torment on the souls deemed condemned.

Murmur: Within the sinister harmonies of the underworld, Murmur stands out as a demon closely linked to music. His influence echoes in every dark chord, summoning melodies that resonate within the hearts of those who wander into the infernal realms. Murmur, the master of demonic symphony, skillfully conducts an orchestra of despair and madness.

Nayla', also known as Nahamay Nhama: is a captivating figure described as a unique succubus who holds a prominent place among the four major female demons in certain esoteric teachings. She is often depicted as the original mother of devils, a title that underscores her immense power and influence in the infernal hierarchy. Her seductive nature and ability to weave powerful enchantments make her a formidable presence. It is said that her charms are not merely physical but also spiritual, captivating both the body and soul of her victims. This dual allure is what draws unwary souls into her grasp, often leading them down a path of darkness and debauchery.

Nabam: Nabam appears as a malevolent demon whose wrath peaks on Saturdays. Irritable and capricious, this dark entity finds delight in burnt bread, perhaps as an offering that fuels its wickedness. During dark rituals, invoking Nabam on a Saturday can unleash his fury, casting hexes that enshroud the charred bread in mysterious infernal plots.

Nebiros, the Lord of the Dead: Within the infernal hierarchy, Nebiros stands as the Leader of the Necromancers, the right hand of the fallen angel Lucifer. This formidable being holds the title of Marshal of the Infernal Militia, bestowed upon him by Lucifer himself. It is said that Nebiros possesses the gift of foresight and the ability to weave evil at his will over those who fall under his gaze. His knowledge spans the magical properties of metals, plants, and minerals, granting him wisdom that transcends the earthly realm.

Nejustán: In biblical accounts, Nejustán emerges as a lesser demon mentioned in the sacred scriptures. His presence weaves through tales of evil and temptation, though the Bible does not delve into specific details about this infernal being.

Nékir, also known as Nechir: also known as Nechir: Nékir is a formidable black angel, whose very presence instills fear in the hearts of those who encounter him. He, along with his ominous companion Munkir, resides in Adhab Algab—the dreaded Islamic purgatory where the souls of the wicked are brought to face their punishment. Together, they serve as enforcers of divine retribution, acting as the fearsome gatekeepers of this dark realm. Nékir's role goes beyond mere torment; he is a relentless judge who interrogates the souls of the deceased, probing their sins and uncovering their darkest deeds.

Nembroth, also known as Mambroth and Naimbroth: This demon is sought by sorcerers specifically on Tuesdays, a day imbued with a particular energy deemed ideal for summoning this ominous entity. The farewell to Nembroth is an intriguing ritual: the act of throwing a small stone at him, a symbolic gesture that severs the magical connection with this demon of hidden knowledge.

Nemesis: In the Greek pantheon, Nemesis stands as a formidable deity, the goddess of vengeance and distributive justice. Her presence echoes the very essence of cosmic fairness, tasked with rewarding virtue and punishing transgression. With her unwavering gaze, Nemesis steers the flow of divine justice, ensuring that every act is met with its rightful consequence.

Nergal, also known as Nirgal: From the shadows of Sumerian and Babylonian mythologies, Nergal, also called Nirgal, emerges as a god of the underworld and lord of the dead. His sinister presence intertwines with the darker aspect of the sun god Shamash. Ruling the underworld alongside his consort, Ereshkigal, Nergal embodies pestilence, fever, and devastation. His attributes—the sickle and the mace—symbolize his dominion over life and death.

Nibhan: Within the passages of the Bible, Nibhan is revealed as a demon of Hebrew mythology. Though mentioned only briefly, his presence casts a shadow over the biblical narratives. As an entity dwelling in darkness, Nibhan embodies temptation and the malevolent influence that lurks in the most unexpected moments.

Nigrum: In the shadowy tales of Europe, Nigrum appears as a cunning demon often depicted in the guise of a black cat, a raven, and, on rare occasions, a man with the head of a stag. His ability to take on various forms allows him to deceive humans, leading them to believe they have dominion over him. However, this illusory pact crumbles in the end, as Nigrum, in his truly malevolent nature, claims the souls of those who fell for his trickery. In a sinister twist, these souls are offered to Belial, weaving a web of demonic intrigue.

Nina: Within Babylonian myths, Nina rises as both a goddess and a she-devil, taking the sinuous form of a serpent. In her reptilian manifestation, Nina embodies the duality of deities, straddling the realms of the divine and the infernal. Her presence is steeped in intrigue and seduction, revealing a divine aspect that transcends conventional notions of good and evil. With her serpentine essence, Nina adds a dark layer to Babylonian mythological narratives, solidifying her place among the mysteries of the underworld.

Nisroch: An enigmatic figure whose origins intertwine with the domain of fallen principalities and the Assyrian deity of agriculture. While commonly associated with Belphegor, his story becomes more intricate when considering his connection to Kenel, a pair of demons ancestrally revered by Mesopotamian cultures. The Assyrians and Chaldeans, in an attempt to mask their darker intentions, worshiped Nisroch and Kenel. Their presence was seemingly pivotal in group sexual rituals, with their invocation believed to be essential for the success of any orgy. Nevertheless, their mutual bond, seemingly harmonious and thriving, defies conventional paradigms, leaving their critics perplexed.

It is whispered that their insatiable nature drives them beyond the normative boundaries of mutual devotion, yet some more balanced critics praise their singular example of unrestricted love. Their possible link to Nimrod, the ancient king mentioned in the Bible, adds additional layers of mystery and speculation to the complex story of Nisroch and Kenel.

Ob: In Syrian folklore, Ob emerges as a unique demon, gifted with the peculiar ability to act as an infernal ventriloquist. His dominion extends beyond conventional shadows, as he can speak through any orifice of the human body. This astonishing, albeit macabre, talent makes him an intriguing figure, evoking both awe and fear. Syrian legends weave his story into tales of demonic possessions and manifestations through human hosts, granting Ob a prominent place among infernal beings.

Oiellet: A prince of the Dominions, Oiellet is a tempting figure who carries the allure of wealth. His mastery lies in his ability to entice men into breaking their vows of poverty, making him the demon of material prosperity. Invoked in Sabbat litanies, Oiellet awakens the most covetous desires and unbridled ambition, weaving his influence into the hearts and minds of those who seek riches at any cost. His presence, subtle yet beguiling, serves as an invitation to betray ethical principles in pursuit of infernal opulence.

Orobas: A powerful Great Prince of Hell, Orobas exudes an aura of mystery and profound knowledge within the realm of demonology. Commanding twenty legions of demons, he possesses the ability to provide accurate answers regarding past, present, and future events, as well as the divine and the creation of the world.

What sets Orobas apart is his unwavering loyalty to the magician who summons him. He resists the temptations of other spirits and never seeks to deceive those who call upon him. Instead, he bestows favors from friends and foes alike and grants honors to those who seek his guidance.

A distinctive feature of Orobas is his chameleon-like appearance. He appears as a majestic horse, but at the request of the magician, he can transform into a human form, which emphasizes his ability to adapt and guide with wisdom.

It is speculated that his name, Orobas, has links to the Latin 'orobias', which refers to a type of incense, which could indicate his association with rituals and magical practices. Furthermore, correspondences with the minor arcana of the tarot, in particular with the 3 of pentacles, highlight his influence during the first days of January. Ultimately, Orobas manifests as a being of knowledge, loyalty, and guidance in the mysterious world of demonology.

Orthon: In the shadowy annals of French folklore, Orthon emerges as a demon of mysterious origin, whose presence is deeply intertwined with acts of possession. His dark influence is recounted in tales of those who fell under his sway during the 19th century. Within the satanic-masonic cult of Palladism, Orthon is revered as a mysterious and enigmatic figure. His aura of intrigue casts a veil over possessions and occult practices, securing him a place within the shadows of satanic and masonic history.

Ovahiche: Among the arts of the troubadours, Ovahiche stands as a patron demon, bestowing exceptional gifts in the craft of rhyme, improvisation, and mastery of the guitar. Troubadours, inspired by Ovahiche's influence, are graced with extraordinary talents that captivate their audiences. This demon, far from sinister shadows, presents himself as a dark patron for those immersed in the world of art and music. His presence elevates the arts but also weaves a thread of dark influence among artists seeking to perfect their craft.

Paimon: The dark monarch of the abyss, Paimon is a second king under Lucifer's dominion. With unyielding loyalty, he bends his will only to the Prince of Darkness, standing steadfast against any other infernal demon or king. This demon, commander of demonic legions, leads 200 legions of lesser demons—or perhaps slightly fewer, depending on the texts. These subordinates carry out his commands and spread across the shadowy realm like an army of nightmares.

In his terrifying form, Paimon appears crowned, riding a dromedary, and wielding a spear—a chilling vision that freezes the souls of those who dare summon his power. Yet, he can alter his appearance, adapting to the needs or preferences of those who call upon him.

Among the abilities and gifts attributed to this lord of the abyss are the teaching of occult arts and sciences, the revelation of dark secrets, the provision of riches, and the granting of dignities. In addition, he is invoked to guide magicians and occultists in their rituals, allowing them to communicate with other spirits and entities from the unfathomable depths. The ceremonies and rituals to attract his attention are somber and disconcerting, and should not be taken lightly. Paimon is one of the most enigmatic and terrifying figures in the underworld, and only the brave or foolish dare to invoke his power in search of knowledge and fortune in the dark confines of the occult.

Paxhet: Feline devil of minor rank in Egyptian religion.

Pazuzu: The brooding king of the wind demons, he emerges from the depths of Sumerian, Assyrian and Akkadian mythology. As the son of the god Hanbi, he inspires both fear and fascination in the ancient narratives of these cultures. In Sumerian tradition, Pazuzu personifies the southwest wind, a force of nature that brings with it storms and unleashes the fury of Mother Nature. His figure is associated with the deity that causes havoc and natural disasters.

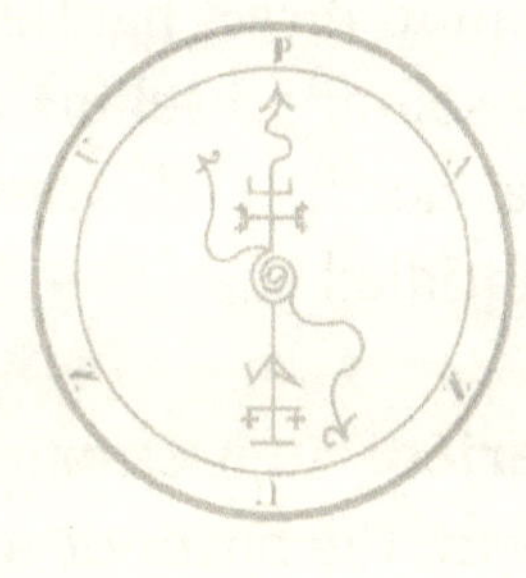

Pazuzu's iconography is equally disturbing, with his grotesque and terrifying face, a mix of human and animal features, including horns, wings and claws. This visual representation reinforces the idea of a supernatural and malevolent being lurking in the shadows, always ready to unleash its power upon the world.

Pazuzu: The influence of Pazuzu extends far beyond the realm of weather. This demon is also a harbinger of plague, pestilence, and disease, plunging humanity into anguish and suffering. He is credited with inducing delirium and fever, making him a terrifying presence that lurks in the darkest moments of life. Pazuzu's dual nature—as a force that governs destructive winds and spreads sickness—reflects ancient beliefs in unseen powers capable of bringing both devastation and healing. His figure serves as a stark reminder of humanity's fragility in the face of uncontrollable elements and illnesses.

Peralda: Peralda reigns as a demon whose domain encompasses the very air itself. His influence unleashes deadly storms, driving hurricanes and cyclones that sweep the land with relentless fury. He collaborates with other demons—Nicksa to summon torrential rains, Gob to spread infectious diseases, and Djim to direct lightning strikes to wreak havoc and death. From his solitary dwelling atop the peaks of the eastern mountains to the north and west, Peralda watches with disdain as his unbridled passion—wrath—erupts in devastating tempests.

Perico: In German demonic lore, Perico emerges as a dark dwarf, the buyer of souls at the hour of death. His grim presence manifests at the bedsides of the dying, offering sinister deals and shadowy pacts. As a cunning being, Perico preys on moments of greatest vulnerability, purchasing souls at a price only the desperate and damned would dare to accept. His dwarfish figure, steeped in shadow, personifies the inevitable darkness that looms at the threshold between life and death.

Phenex (Phenes): The Grand Marquis of Hell, is a mysterious and awe-inspiring entity in demonology. Commanding twenty legions of demons, he holds extraordinary abilities and knowledge beyond human comprehension. What sets Phenes apart is his unparalleled command over the wondrous sciences, a realm of wisdom that extends far beyond the earthly plane. Furthermore, he is renowned for his exceptional poetic talent, able to craft verses that enchant and astonish.

However, his obedience to the mage who summons him stands out as one of his most remarkable traits. Phenes submits to the will of the conjurer, placing himself at their service. Yet, Phenes harbors an intriguing secret: his longing to return to Heaven after 1,200 years. This hope, however, seems futile, as he deceives himself with this illusion. This ambiguity raises questions about the nature of his existence and his true desires.

The physical manifestation of Phenes is equally captivating. He appears as a phoenix, a legendary creature known for its ability to rise from its ashes. His voice, childlike in tone, sings sweet melodies, yet this song should not be heard, for it may lead to unintended consequences. The mage who summons him must not be alone, for Phenes cannot remain solitary. Over time, it is said, this demon transforms into a human, raising further questions about his ever-evolving nature. With his mysterious powers, his yearning to return to Heaven, and his duality between phoenix and human form, Phenes becomes an enigma in the world of demonology.

Rabisu ('the stalker,' the wanderer) or Habisú: In the rich Assyrian-Babylonian mythology, Rabisu, also known as Habisú, emerges as a demon whose appearances are as unpredictable as they are unsettling. This wandering being lurks in dark corners, stalking and sowing chaos within human homes. His presence evokes terror, sending shivers down the spines of those unfortunate enough to glimpse him. Rabisu delights in causing confusion and disturbance, embodying the darkness that hides within unpredictable shadows.
Radna: Forged from the hatred, vanity, envy, lust, gluttony, sloth, and greed of humankind.

He rises as a demon forged from the worst manifestations of the seven deadly sins. As the king of demons, his insatiable hunger is directed toward the blood and hearts of creatures. Capable of absorbing his foes and replicating their appearance and abilities, Radna personifies the evil born of human vices. A fearsome entity that feeds on the darkness residing in the impious hearts.

Rahab: Within the lower demon hierarchy, Rahab stands out as the prince of the oceans. In the watery depths, his dominion stretches over the seas, revealing a power that defies the apparent calm of the waters. Though his presence is lesser compared to other demons, it embodies the relentless force of the dark currents that lie beneath the surface of the vast ocean.

Raküti: A demon of unknown origin, depicted with two heads, rises as the overseer of the wheel of fortune. This wheel, like a cosmic roulette, marks the randomness of good or bad luck in the lives of humans. Raküti is said to possess the power to control fate, manipulating the fickle turns of this wheel. With his two heads, he symbolizes the duality of human experience, where fortune and misfortune intertwine in an unpredictable dance.

Rāvana: In Hindu mythology, Rāvana stands as a formidable demon with ten heads and ten pairs of arms. This colossal being defied the gods and ruled with an iron fist until he was finally defeated by the god Rāma. The complexity of his many heads symbolizes the intricate nature of evil, and his defeat by Rāma represents the triumph of virtue over dark forces.

Ronove: Distinguished as a Marquis and Grand Earl of Hell, his mastery encompasses the arts of rhetoric and language, granting him persuasive and manipulative skills. This scheming demon has the ability to provide good servants and favors to both friends and enemies, revealing a duality that goes beyond the typical notions of good and evil.

Though descriptions of his appearance may be vague, his association with soul harvesting adds a dark undertone to his nature. Ronove engages in the harvesting of souls from elderly individuals and animals near death, weaving his influence into the critical moments between life and transition to the underworld. The combination of his skills in the art of speech and soul harvesting grants him a unique and enigmatic role in the infernal hierarchy. His presence, shrouded in mystery, reveals a being that goes beyond simple malevolence, exploring the complexities of demonic nature.

RONOVE

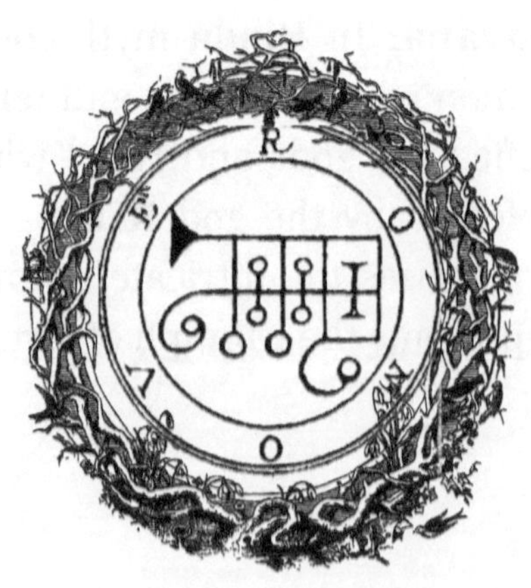

Sabnock: The enigmatic Sabnock rises from the depths of Hell like a Great Marquis, commanding a host of fifty legions of demons. His presence evokes an eerie feeling, as if the shadows themselves close in on him.

This dark being has a particularly sinister ability, building tall towers, castles and cities, fortifying them with weapons and ammunition. But he does not stop at creation, he also enjoys causing suffering to mortals. He can inflict terrible wounds, gangrenous sores and fill them with maggots, a torment that lasts for days. His appearance is a monstrous combination: a warrior in armor and weapons, the head of a lion and riding a horse as pale as death. This sinister, disturbing and mysterious figure illustrates the dark and destructive side of the demonic world.

SABNOCK

Sabazios, Sabazis, Sabacio, or Sabasius: In the shadows of Phrygian folklore, Sabazios emerges as a distinguished demon, leader of the witches' Sabbat. His unsettling depiction includes horns, a blood-stained phallus, and a serpent as his emblem. Sabazios is often associated with Bendis or Cotys, and linked to the Greek deities Dionysus and the Roman Bacchus. This blend of mythologies suggests a demonic figure that embodies intoxication, sexuality, and hidden rituals.

Sakar: An infernal genius who—according to the Talmud—lies in the lake of Tiberias, bound by a stone around his neck as punishment.

Samael: Enigmatic and powerful, Samael rises as a multifaceted archangel in the rich Talmudic and post-Talmudic tradition. His name, translating to "Poison of God" or "Blindness of God," reflects his duality and complexity. Often, Samael is identified as the accuser or adversary, a role akin to Satan in Christian tradition, though his nature is not necessarily malevolent. This archangel is also the seducer and the angel of destruction, with roles both protective and devastating. He is credited with the destruction of sinners, which can ultimately be seen as a beneficial act, purifying the world. Samael, ruler of the Fifth Heaven and one of the seven regents of the world, is served by countless angels and resides in the Seventh Heaven. His functions in Jewish mythology are varied and often dark. He is the chief angel of death and leader of the satans, linking him to the shadow of human mortality.

In some narratives, Samael plays a significant role in the story of the Garden of Eden, often associated with the temptation of Adam and Eve.

He is also credited with being the father of Cain and is considered the partner of Lilith. However, he is not always identified with Satan, and this connection was developed in later writings.

Samael is a complex being, ranging from purification through destruction to the shadow of deception and temptation. In some Gnostic cosmologies, he is identified as the Demiurge, the source of evil and the creator of the material world, which contrasts with his role in the Jewish tradition, where he remains a servant of God.

Samamiel: A high-ranking demon in Constantinople, whose preference was for blonde women.

Samyazza, also known as Semjaza, Semihazah, Shemhazai, or Samjâzâ: Is a prominent figure in the mythology of the fallen angels. He is part of a group known as the Grigori, "watcher" angels who rebelled against God. Semyazza leads these fallen angels and plays a pivotal role in their story.

The tale recounts how the Grigori, tempted by carnal desires for mortal women, became fallen angels due to their lack of self-control. Semyazza took primary responsibility for their actions, but his fellow Grigori shared in his punishment. In total, about two hundred fallen angels descended upon Mount Hermon, also known as Ardis. These celestial beings united with mortal women and fathered giants, described as colossal creatures reaching "three thousand cubits in height each." The Grigori also committed other sins, such as revealing the secrets of warfare to mortals, which led to widespread destruction and violence.

These giants, known as the Nephilim (meaning "the fallen ones"), turned into malevolent beings who ruled over beasts and humans alike. Their existence brought widespread corruption to the Earth. To end this corruption, God sent the angel Gabriel to battle the Nephilim. Once they were defeated, God unleashed the Great Flood, eradicating most living creatures on Earth, sparing only Noah, his family, and a pair of each animal species.

The punishment of Semyazza and the Grigori was that they would remain bound to the Earth for seventy generations, or until the Day of Judgment. On that day, they would be cast into the fiery abyss to endure eternal torment.

The tale of Semyazza and the Grigori is a fascinating account that reveals the fall of the angels and their role in the myth of the Great Flood. It also emphasizes the struggle between carnal desire and divine obedience, culminating in the eternal damnation of these fallen beings.

Saracil: In the realms of mythology and demonology, Saracil stands out as one of the three demons known as the Divi. These beings, who dwell near the Moon, hold dominion over both land and sea. Their influence is most potent during dark nights, exerting power over the elements and the vast expanse of the oceans.

Sargatanas: Bearing the title of Brigadier of the Infernal Militia, Sargatanas is depicted as a powerful demon. His attributes include mastery over invisibility and the ability to teach human cunning and secret sciences. As the leader of Hell's militias, his influence extends through the shadows and the arcane knowledge of the occult.

Sathariel: An archdevil within Kabbalistic tradition, Sathariel is characterized by his obstruction of divine mercy. Within the intricate framework of Kabbalistic beliefs, he emerges as a figure that darkens divine compassion, working against benevolent principles.

Sathiel (Sariel): Also known as Sariel, Sathiel is a high-ranking demon and one of the Divi or superior beings. As the Prince of the Moon, his dominion encompasses nocturnal mysteries and lunar energies. His association with Aamon suggests a collaboration within the demonic hierarchy, where these superior beings fulfill specific roles in a dark cosmogony.

Shax: A Marquis of demonology, Shax exudes an aura both intriguing and dangerous. He commands thirty legions of demons and wields influence over sight, hearing, and human understanding when invoked.

Under his command, he can steal money from kings and kings of houses, promising to return it within 1,200 years. In addition, Shax is engaged in stealing horses and other desires from those who summon him. But beware, Shax is known for his cunning and ability to deceive.

Though he is considered loyal and obedient, his true nature is one of deception. Only those who force him into a magical triangle can get him to reveal the truth. In that confined space, Shax will speak "beautifully" and provide truthful answers. But beyond that triangle, he is a master in the art of deception and lying.

The aura of mystery surrounding Shax, his ability to sense and steal whatever you desire, and his cunning nature make this demon a dangerous being in demonology. Any interaction with him should be undertaken with extreme caution and knowledge.

Seddim: A demon associated with destructive power, Seddim stands out within the dark hierarchy of infernal entities. His essence is tied to chaos and annihilation, embodying the ability to unleash cataclysmic forces upon the universe.

Sira (Seera, Sire): Sira emerges as a formidable demonic prince under the command of Amaymon. His appearance is that of a handsome man mounted on a winged horse, symbolizing majesty and swiftness in his form. As a master of time, Sira possesses the ability to manipulate temporal perception, either accelerating or slowing down time at will. He also wields the power of instantaneous transportation, moving objects or beings across vast distances in an instant. Sira's presence suggests a being with dominion over fundamental aspects of the universe, manifesting his might through the control of time and space.

Sidragaso: The lord of the infernal duchy of Lagneia, Sidragaso is a sinister and grotesque figure in demonology. His physical form is terrifying—a leopard's face, a human torso, goat-like legs, a scorpion's tail, and raven's wings combine to create a truly nightmarish being. He is surrounded by exquisite fragrances that stir sexual desire in women, and his gift for charming words makes him particularly dangerous.

Sidragaso's purpose is to seduce women, convincing them they are the most beautiful and luring them into lascivious and orgiastic activities during demonic gatherings such as the Sabbath. His goal is to amplify carnal desires in men and encourage acts of fornication. A master manipulator, Sidragaso uses his skills to ensnare his victims in a web of lust and depravity.

He is held responsible for promoting debauchery and pornography across Europe, as illustrated in the tale of Sylvia and Günther. In this story, Sidragaso persuades Sylvia to expose her nakedness before a group of men in pursuit of material gain. However, her ambition leads to a tragic fate: the conception of a deformed child and her own death during childbirth. In demonology, Sidragaso embodies seduction and corruption, his actions leaving devastation in their wake.

Sitri: In demonology, Sitri is a demon with a sinister purpose. He commands thirty legions of demons and appears as a grotesque figure, with the body of a man, a terrifying face, and razor-sharp claws. His most dangerous trait, however, is his ability to influence and seduce human hearts. A master manipulator, Sitri wields the power to ignite uncontrollable sexual desire in people, driving them to abandon reason. His ultimate goal is to awaken carnal passions and lure individuals into acts of lust and depravity. A skilled tempter, he preys on human frailties, pushing his victims to surrender to their darkest desires.

Like other demons of lust, Sitri seeks pleasure at the expense of morality and ethics. He is summoned to fulfill carnal desires and satisfy humanity's basest impulses. His actions can lead to devastating consequences, as he incites individuals to act against their own principles and values.

SITRI

Sorath: Under Lucifer's command, Sorath emerges as the entity who rules over the 616 stars of death. This demonic figure carries an aura of darkness and destruction, being an integral part of the infernal retinue that follows Lucifer, the Prince of Darkness.

Tartac (Tartak): In Hebrew mythology, Tartac, also known as Tartak, is a demon mentioned in several passages of the Bible. In Kutha, he was worshiped as the god of the wind by the Assyrian settlers of Samaria. His connection to the wind suggests a figure embodying natural forces, while also being linked to pagan practices.

Tefnet (Tefnut): A lesser demon in Egyptian mythology, Tefnet takes the form of a she-devil with the head of a lioness. As the sister and consort of Shu, she personifies the element of moisture and embodies the dangers of feminine seduction. Her presence highlights duality in mythology, representing both fertility and peril.

Tetal : A Chaldean demon, Tetal channels his power into the possession and deterioration of hands and arms in humans. His sinister essence manifests through physical harm, reflecting his ability to cause distress and suffering via malignant possession.

Thaumiel: In Kabbalistic tradition, Thaumiel rises as an archdemon who sought to be equal to God. His rebellion and desire to attain divine status reveal the ambition and arrogance that define this infernal figure within the Kabbalistic cosmology.

Titi: An intriguing figure in Babylonian mythology, Titi is often described as a demon princess who personifies the essence of Chaos demons and pagan worship. Her dominion extends over saltwater, an element commonly associated with the mysterious and enigmatic nature of the unknown.

The physical representation of Titi is equally enigmatic and terrifying. With claws similar to those of a bird of prey and large horns, its appearance is that of a nightmare creature. The presence of two heads in its representations makes it an even more disturbing and unique being.

Titi becomes a figure that evokes both fear and awe. As the goddess of saltwater, her influence and power can be both beneficial and devastating. In Babylonian mythology, Titi embodies the duality of nature, possessing the ability to bring both life and destruction through her dominion.

Togarini: In Kabbalistic tradition, Togarini stands out as an archdemon with a particular influence in the realm of wars. His role is that of an instigator of conflicts and confrontations, carrying with him the essence of discord and violence within the Kabbalistic cosmology.

Tuculca (Tuculcha, Tuchulca): In Etruscan mythology, Tuculca emerges as a fearsome monster of infernal origin. His appearance is a terrifying blend of features: an eagle's beak, donkey ears, serpent hair, a yellowish human body, and bird-like wings and legs. This mythological creation embodies the vivid and often grotesque imagination of ancient cultures.

Unsere: This demon rises as an archdemoness associated with fertility and witchcraft. Her presence shifts between the ability to foster fertility and the practice of mystical arts.

Ufir (Uphir): Stands out as a demon skilled in chemistry. His domain encompasses the knowledge of substances and their application, positioning him as the protector of healers within the infernal hierarchy. Beyond his expertise in chemistry, Ufir also serves as the physician of the underworld, offering his skills to maintain health in the dark realms.

Uzza: Originally an angel, Uzza underwent a transformation into a demon due to his lust for women. His fragile spirit led him down the path of disobedience, and as a result, he was condemned to the demonic state. This tale highlights the fall of a celestial being through spiritual weakness and a temptation for earthly desires, illustrating the moral duality that defines many narratives of fallen angels across different traditions.

Valefor: Is a demon with an unusual and challenging appearance that stretches the imagination. He is represented in two distinct forms, making him a unique and unsettling figure in demonological folklore. In one form, he appears as a lion with the head of a man, creating a terrifying hybrid image that blends beastly and human elements. In his other form, he possesses the head of a donkey, which is even stranger and more disconcerting.

This demon exerts a malignant influence on people, inciting them to commit acts of theft and fostering relationships between criminals. However, his sinister role goes further, as after luring individuals into the world of crime, he drags them into the abyss of hell.

Despite his evil nature, Valefor is known for granting good familiar spirits, which can be considered a contradiction in his demonic nature. While he corrupts some, he also offers a form of spiritual connection to others. Controlling ten legions of demons shows his power and dominance in the underworld.

In tarot tradition, Valefor is related to the 4 of pentacles and spans a period from January 11 to 21, although the exact dates may vary. This zodiacal correspondence adds an additional touch of mystery to his demonic figure.

Vapula: Mighty Grand Duke of Hell, is an intriguing figure in the realm of demonology. With command over thirty-six legions of demons, his authority is undeniable. What makes Vapula particularly fascinating is his ability to teach a wide range of intellectual disciplines. This demon acts as a scholar in the infernal sense, imparting knowledge in fields such as philosophy, mechanics, and the sciences.

The combination of these areas of study gives insight into his ability to delve into knowledge and understand both the mind and the mechanics of the world around him. As for his appearance, Vapula is described as a winged lion with griffin-like features. This form combines elements of the lion's majesty with the ferocity of a griffin, creating an image that inspires both respect and fear.

Vapula's influence extends through his teachings and the authority he wields over legions of demons. His ability to impart wisdom and knowledge in intellectual fields makes him a unique demonic figure in the realm of demonology.

VAPULA

Verrier: Known as the demon of disobedience, Verrier is deeply connected to rebellion and defiance. Beyond his role as an instigator of disobedience, Verrier possesses profound knowledge of herbalism and plants in general. This duality in his abilities highlights the blend of dark and natural elements within his being, suggesting that his influence extends both to the supernatural realm and to earthly wisdom regarding plants.

Verrine: A minor demon, Verrine is depicted as the devil of health and impatience. His dominion spans both the physical and emotional spheres, allowing him to influence an individual's health while also stirring impatience in their hearts. Verrine's presence underscores the connection between physical well-being and emotional states in demonological mythology.

Viné: A Count and King of Hell, Viné stands as a figure of power and revelation. Commanding thirty-six legions of demons, he wields formidable authority in the underworld. His abilities transcend conventional understanding, as he has the power to unveil the secrets of time and space. Viné possesses supernatural insight into the mysteries of the past, present, and future. He is also adept at detecting the hidden, capable of uncovering witches and buried secrets.

Additionally, his power extends to manipulating natural elements; he can conjure storms and unleash the fury of water. In terms of his physical representation, Viné is portrayed as a lion gripping a serpent in his claw while riding a mighty black horse.

As for his physical representation, Viné is portrayed as a lion holding a snake in his claw, while riding on an imposing black horse. This representation symbolizes his mastery and control over ferocity and cunning, manifesting his ability to demolish obstacles and build fortresses with skill.

The etymological origin of his name, which resembles the Latin word "vinea" meaning "vine", evokes both strength and prowess, underlining the fearless and powerful nature of this unique demon in the world of demonology.

Vucub Caquix: In Quiché mythology, specifically in the Popol Vuh, Vucub Caquix emerges as a demon whose figure is imbued with vanity and egolatry. His presence in this ancient Mayan narrative highlights the cultural and mythological richness of the region. According to the Popol Vuh, Vucub Caquix is an arrogant and proud being, characteristics that lead him to suffer consequences in history.

Volac: Within the demonic hierarchy, Volac, also known as Valac, emerges as a Grand President of Hell, commanding authority over a significant number of legions—some sources cite thirty, while others suggest thirty-eight, reflecting the variability often found in demonological accounts.

Volac's power lies in his ability to reveal the location of serpents and bring them under the control of the summoner. This gift allows him to exert dominion over these creatures, compelling them to obey the invoker's commands. His influence even extends to these reptiles, often associated in demonology with deception and venom. Curiously, Volac's appearance is strikingly peculiar and evokes an unusual image. He is described as resembling a modestly dressed young child, with the addition of angelic wings. The imagery becomes even more surreal when he is depicted riding a two-headed dragon. This contradictory representation—combining the innocence of childhood, the majesty of angelic form, and the power of a mythical dragon—adds layers of mystery and intrigue to his persona.
Volac's presence and abilities can be interpreted in various ways, enriching the symbolism and enigma surrounding his role in this dark tradition.

VOLAC

Vairen: Vairen rises as a fallen angel, embodying the essence of rebellion and disobedience. Known as the demon of impulses, his influence manifests through the incitement of unrestrained desires and actions. A breaker of boundaries, Vairen challenges moral and societal constraints, encouraging those under his sway to cross pre-established limits.

Xezbet (Jezebeth, Jesabel, Jezbet, Xerbeth): This demon personifies deceit and falsehood. As the demon of lies, Xezbet specializes in crafting illusions and weaving deception. His domain extends to creating fraudulent miracles and manipulating the perceptions of those who fall under his influence. Xezbet's presence highlights humanity's vulnerability to trickery and the dangers of trusting what appears real but is, in truth, an illusory creation of this cunning demon.

Xaphan: A dark figure in demonological lore, Xaphan is one of the fallen angels who joined Satan's rebellion against God. As a result of his defiance, he was cast into the abyss of Hell, where his role took on a unique and punishing nature. Xaphan earned his place among the fallen through his inventive mind, as his proposal during the celestial revolt was particularly audacious. According to legend, he suggested setting fire to the heavenly realms, a symbolic act of rebellion against God.

However, before this infamous act of celestial arson could be carried out, Xaphan and the other rebellious angels were hurled into Hell. His eternal punishment assigns him a singular role in the infernal domain: to fan the flames of Hell's furnaces with his own mouth and hands. His duty is to keep the tormenting fires of Hell alive and blazing. As a symbol of his task, he is often depicted with a bellows.

Xaphan stands as a grim reminder of the consequences of rebellion and disobedience in demonic mythology, playing a unique role in the underworld by fanning the flames that punish the damned for all eternity. His figure brings an additional dimension to the rich narrative of demonology, where each demon embodies a different aspect of darkness and transgression.

Yama: Yama holds the position of king in the Chinese hell known as Di Yu. This place is an intricate labyrinth of underground dungeons where souls face their punishments in correspondence with the sins committed during their earthly life. The figure of Yama in Chinese mythology reflects the concept of divine justice and postmortem destiny based on the actions of each individual. It is interesting to note the similarity with Yama, the Hindu demigod. Both share the function of judging and punishing souls in the afterlife, although with different cultural nuances. The convergence of these figures highlights the universality of themes such as judgment and destiny after death present in various mythological traditions.

Yekum: Yekum is counted among the fallen angels who, according to tradition, seduced the children of men and descended from heaven. This tale emphasizes the fall of these celestial beings, corrupted by their own inclinations, who led humanity down a path of disobedience and sin. Yekum's story reflects recurring themes in various mythologies about temptation and the downfall of heavenly beings.

Yakshī: In Hindu mythology, Yakshī is portrayed as a succubus demon capable of taking the form of an insatiable, beautiful woman. This seductive entity embodies temptation and lust, entrapping those who fall under her spell. The figure of Yakshī underscores the connection between Hindu mythology and similar representations of seductive beings found across diverse cultures.

Yoma: Within mythology tied to shinobi lore, Yoma is a type of parasitic demon. It originates from the bloodshed between shinobi and is intrinsically linked to the flow of blood within a shinobi barrier. The connection of Yoma to blood and the shinobi barrier highlights elements of Japanese mythology and the symbolic relationship between spilled lifeblood and the emergence of demonic entities.

Zabulón: Zabulón is depicted as a demon associated with gluttony. He is also attributed with characteristics of a lascivious and shameless incubus. This demonic figure embodies the vices of excessive indulgence and uncontrolled lust, illustrating the link between demons and the seven deadly sins in mythology.

Zabulus: Zabulus is an incubus demon who, during the Middle Ages, was believed to be responsible for acts of possession.

Zagan: A monarch and president of the underworld in demonology, he holds dominion over thirty-six legions of demons. His ability to perform astonishing transformations makes him a notable figure in the demonic pantheon. One of Zagan's most distinctive abilities is his ability to transform substances. He can turn wine into water, water into wine, and even more remarkably, blood into wine. Additionally, he possesses the power to transmute metals into coins made of the same metal, which has significant practical implications.

His visual representation is intriguing, as he is described as having a human body, but with the head of a bull and wings resembling those of a griffin. This unique appearance reflects his dual nature, combining human elements with traits from mythology and the beast. Zagan adds an enigmatic element to the complex world of demonic beliefs and depictions.

Zaurón: Zaurón emerges as a demon within Mazdean religion, regarded as the god of theft and murder. Under the influence of Ahriman, the evil entity in Zoroastrianism, Zaurón acts as a tempter, particularly targeting kings to incite tyranny. His figure embodies corruption and the seduction towards malevolent deeds, playing a pivotal role in the cosmic struggle between the forces of good and evil in Mazdean mythology.

Zimiar (Zymyar): Zimiar, also known as Zymyar, holds a prominent position in the infernal hierarchy as one of the kings of Hell, ruling over the northern regions of the underworld. His domain, described as a vast expanse of icy darkness and desolation, is associated with perpetual suffering and the forlorn state of the damned souls dwelling in those lands.

Zimiar is not merely a figure of power but also a shrewd and calculating strategist in the eternal struggle between chaos and creation. Many accounts suggest his influence extends beyond the underworld, reaching into the realm of the living. Here, he sows discord in human hearts and manipulates leaders and rulers to succumb to corruption and tyranny.

Often depicted as an imposing sovereign, wearing a crown forged of black flames and wielding a scepter of crystallized ice, Zimiar symbolizes the duality of his domain: the deadly cold that paralyzes and the blazing wrath that consumes. His role in demonological lore highlights the intricate structure of the underworld—not just as a place of torment but also as an organized realm where each ruler fulfills a specific purpose in administering eternal punishment.

The hierarchy of demons is a concept found primarily in Christian demonology, and is based on the classification of these evil beings according to their supposed power and rank in the underworld. It is important to note that these hierarchies are not universally accepted and vary in detail depending on the sources. One of the best-known hierarchies is that derived from works such as "The Lesser Key of Solomon" and "The Greater Key of Solomon", which are medieval grimoires.

HERE IS A SIMPLIFIED VERSION OF A COMMON DEMONIC HIERARCHY

1) Lucifer/Satan: Considered the supreme leader of demons, he is often associated with rebellion against God.

2) Princes of Hell: These are high-ranking demons who rule over specific regions of the underworld. Some examples include Beelzebub, Asmodeus, and Mephistopheles.

3) Marquises, Dukes and Counts: Mid-ranking demons who have authority over legions of lesser demons. Examples include Bael, Stolas and Furfur.

4) Knights, Presidents, and Princes: Another layer of demons that exert control over smaller groups. For example, Barbatos, Gremory, and Orobas.

5) Infernal Marquises and Counts: Demons of lower rank but still have influence and power. Examples include Aamon and Buer.

6) Infernal Knights and Ministers: Demons of lower rank, often associated with specific tasks or functions. For example, Agares and Vassago.

7) Infernal Servants: The lowest ranking demons that perform the most basic tasks. These can include various demonic creatures and evil spirits.

Although exploring the hierarchies of demons and their roles in Christian demonology is fascinating, it is important to acknowledge that these structures lack a direct basis in the Bible. Instead, they are theological and mystical constructs that have evolved throughout history, shaped by diverse intellectual currents and cultural contexts.

These interpretations vary widely depending on the source and tradition. In some cases, additional sinister details emerge, such as the association of certain demons with specific practices, cursed objects, or dark rituals. Demonology, in its complexity, has often inspired dark tales and myths that fuel humanity's enduring fascination with the supernatural and the malevolent.

It is essential to note that these ideas are deeply rooted in Christian demonology and are not universal across all beliefs about supernatural or malevolent beings. Different religions and cultural traditions have their own conceptions of evil and malicious entities, which can differ significantly from Christian depictions. This diversity of interpretations adds further layers of mystery and horror to the rich history of beliefs surrounding the demonic.

RELATIONSHIP BETWEEN DEMONS AND PAGAN DEITIES

Pan (Grecia):

The Greek god of the forests, shepherds, and untamed nature.

Connection to Demons: The often grotesque image of Pan influenced Christian depictions of demons associated with evil.
Pan embodies the archetypal manifestation of wild nature, dancing in the shadows of ancient Greece. This pantheistic deity, intertwined with the essence of the forests and pastoral life, evokes undeniable fascination in the hearts of those seeking the hidden mysteries within the folds of Hellenic mythology. With his shaggy legs, goat-like horns, and magical flute echoing through the breeze, Pan personifies the bridge between divine and earthly realms.

His eyes gleam with the spark of the primal, and his laughter reverberates like the echoes of the most remote and sacred places. In tranquil woodlands and the depths of mystical caves, Pan appears as the free spirit governing fertility and the animal kingdom. To call upon Pan is to unlock the gates to nature's untamed vitality, to immerse oneself in the eternal dance of creation, and to feel the divine energy coursing through the earth.

Under the light of a full moon, Pan reveals the secrets of the wild, guiding those who seek ancient wisdom and a connection to the primal facets of existence. His mythological figure, with its enchanting yet fearsome duality, stands as a beacon in the vast sea of the occult, inviting seekers of the mysterious to delve into the realms of pagan divinity.

Cernunnos (Celta):

The Celtic god associated with fertility, animals, and the untamed wild.

Connection to Demons: His horned, animalistic appearance was reinterpreted as demonic in certain Christian contexts.

Cernunnos embodies the very essence of the magic woven into the ancient Celtic tapestry. With his majestic image, part man and part stag, he reveals the sacred connection between the human realm and the natural world. In his antlers and piercing gaze lies the ancestral wisdom of the forests, the vitality of fertility, and the untamed spirit of wildlife. To invoke Cernunnos is to open the doors to the earth's secrets, to immerse oneself in the cosmic dance of existence, and to feel the universe's pulse in every fiber of one's being.

Under the glow of the moon, Cernunnos leads those who seek communion with the divine in nature, unraveling the mysteries of creation and renewal. He is the lord of the forests, the guardian of eternal cycles, and in his presence, ancient magic awakens, whispering lost secrets through the rustling leaves and the shadows of the night.

Hecate (Greece)

Goddess associated with magic, witchcraft, and crossroads.

Connection to Demons: In later accounts, Hecate became linked to demonic practices and dark magic.

Hecate, queen of crossroads and enchantress of the night in Greek mythology, evokes an unfathomable fascination. With her triple-faced form watching over the divergent paths of fate, she embodies mastery over magic, dark moons, and moments of transition and change. To call upon her is to delve into the mysteries of witchcraft and connect with hidden realms.

Under the cloak of the moon, Hecate, your torches illuminate the paths of esoteric knowledge, revealing truths in the shadows and guiding those who seek mystical wisdom. You are the goddess of mysteries, the guardian of ancient secrets, and in your presence, magic flows like a dark river, winding through the veils that separate worlds. In the silent hours of the night, Hecate, you rise as the mistress of the occult, spreading your wings over seekers of the unknown. At the crossroads of the sacred and the profane, you are the guide who unveils truth beyond appearances. O Hecate, in your complex and enigmatic form, echoes the call to explore the deepest recesses of the occult and uncover the secrets that dwell in the shadows.

Krampus (Alpine Mythology)

A figure rooted in Alpine mythology, closely tied to Christmas traditions. Connection to Demons: In modern interpretations, Krampus is often portrayed as a demonic companion to Santa Claus. This legendary being, steeped in Alpine traditions, emerges as the diabolical counterpart to the festive joy of Christmas. With twisted horns and a bifurcated tongue, Krampus embodies the wild and untamed aspects of nature. His presence is both a warning and a reminder of the duality of the season, blending revelry with retribution. Krampus stands as a stark contrast to Saint Nicholas, a shadowy figure who reinforces the balance between reward and punishment during the winter celebrations.

Krampus's sinister mission—to punish naughty children—reveals a darker side to festive celebrations. To invoke the figure of Krampus is to immerse oneself in the mysteries of pagan beliefs, where the sacred and the profane intertwine in an eternal dance. On the icy nights of December, Krampus becomes Santa Claus's dark companion, a reminder that light and shadow coexist in the very fabric of reality. The tradition of Krampus, with its blend of folklore and symbolism, echoes ancient pagan beliefs that endure in modern festivities. This Christmas demon, with his clinking chains and basket to carry away disobedient children, serves as both a harbinger of hidden lessons and a link to the archaic roots of holiday celebrations.

O Krampus, you weave diabolical charm with the magic of the season, reminding us that even in the radiant light of Christmas, shadows dance on the edges of our perception.

Pomba Gira (Candomblé y Umbanda, Brasil):

A feminine spirit associated with sensuality and love in certain Afro-Brazilian traditions. Connection to Demons: Often misinterpreted as a demonic entity due to cultural misunderstandings and religious stigmatization.

Pomba Gira, the Afro-Brazilian deity, stirs my deepest intrigue within the vast landscape of the occult. Shrouded in mystery, this entity embodies sensuality and feminine power within the spiritual frameworks of Umbanda and Quimbanda. Pomba Gira, la divinidad afrobrasileña que despierta mi intriga más profunda en el vasto panorama del ocultismo. Con su presencia envuelta en misterio, esta entidad es la personificación de la sensualidad y el poder femenino en la cosmovisión de la Umbanda y la Quimbanda.

Her presence is a testament to the resilience of ancestral traditions, where the duality of passion and wisdom merges into an unbreakable force. Pomba Gira's energy is magnetic, drawing seekers into the realm of self-discovery and empowerment. She symbolizes liberation, transformation, and the unyielding strength of femininity, challenging societal norms and embracing the fluidity of identity and desire.

To honor Pomba Gira is to recognize the sanctity of the feminine divine, to celebrate the beauty of self-expression, and to delve into the enigmatic realms where spirituality meets earthly pleasures. She stands as a beacon for those who seek to reclaim their power and forge a path through the crossroads of life, defying convention and embracing the infinite possibilities of existence.

To invoke Pomba Gira is to immerse oneself in the mysteries of sacred sexuality and the connection to the spiritual plane. Under the full moon, Pomba Gira emerges as the guardian of hidden desires and the protector of those who seek freedom in love. Her ritual dance, brimming with allure and magnetism, unveils the potent energy radiating from overflowing femininity.

In the embrace of the night, Pomba Gira reigns as the queen of desire, defying conventions and igniting the eternal flame of passion. O Pomba Gira, your presence at the crossroads of the divine and the earthly resonates as a call to delve into the depths of feminine magic and the spiritual connection that transcends the boundaries of the known world!

Apep (Egyptian Mythology)

A chaotic serpent who embodied darkness and chaos.

Connection to Demons: In some modern interpretations, Apep is compared to demonic entities due to his chaotic nature.

The cosmic serpent that slithers through the shadows of Egyptian mythology, you awaken my deepest fascination. Your sinuous body slides between the layers of time and space, embodying the eternal antagonist of the sun god Ra. You personify the chaos and darkness that threaten to devour the divine light of the sun.

To invoke your name is to plunge into the mysteries of cosmic duality, where the eternal struggle between creation and destruction unfolds in a celestial ballet. In your presence, the very fabric of existence trembles, caught in the dance of balance and annihilation. Apep, you are both a destroyer and a force of necessary chaos, revealing the profound truth that all things must be torn down before they can be reborn.

Under the cloak of the starry night, Apep, you rise as the very embodiment of the chaotic forces lurking in the depths of the universe. You are the antithesis of divine order, defying the cosmic structure with your imposing presence. In Egyptian mythology, your image as the great serpent dwelling in the primordial waters serves as a constant reminder of the fragility of balance in the cosmos.

O Apep, in your serpentine shadow, I glimpse the essence of primordial chaos, a reminder that in the depths of occultism and mythology, darkness and light dance together in an eternal and inscrutable waltz.

Barbatos (Western Demonology)

Inspired by Pan and other nature gods.

Connection to Demons: In Western demonology, Barbatos is a demon mentioned in medieval grimoires.

The mysterious entity that slips between the veils of pagan spirituality, Barbatos ignites my fascination with his enigmatic presence. In the pantheon of ancient deities, this being manifests as a wise guide to the hidden secrets of nature, a custodian of the connection between the visible and the invisible worlds.

I envision Barbatos as a figure in the twilight of ancestral forests, his dominion extending through the oldest and most sacred corners of the earth. Under his influence, the whispers of nature reveal the intertwined threads of destiny and the wisdom flowing from the very roots of knowledge.

As the guardian of the natural realms, Barbatos offers those who seek his guidance a deeper connection with the earth and its unfathomable mysteries. His presence invites one to listen to the ancient rhythms of nature, where the unseen energies of the world converge. In his wisdom, the secrets of the forests, the winds, and the stars come to life, weaving together the forgotten knowledge of the ages. To walk in the path of Barbatos is to embrace the primal force that links all life, understanding that the land holds not only the roots of existence but the answers to the questions whispered by the universe itself.

WITCHCRAFT AND DEMONOLOGY:

HISTORY

Through the clandestine corridors of history, where witchcraft and demonology dance in a macabre waltz of mysteries and ancestral fears. In the dark folds of the Middle Ages and the Inquisition, a veil of paranoia hangs over Europe, and the witch hunt rages like an unholy storm, pushing humanity towards the abyss of the unknown.

In the centuries where shadows were silent accomplices, witchcraft became a forbidden whisper among mortals. In the darkness of those days, demonology built its invisible networks, interweaving forbidden beliefs and dark pacts in the parchment of existence. The very air vibrated with the echo of spells and the fear of the supernatural loomed like an insatiable spectre.

As the Middle Ages become a bubbling cauldron of superstition, witch hunters, wielding dogma and torches, unleash a merciless pursuit. Accusations, like long shadows, are cast over those identified as carriers of witchcraft, condemning them to the thin line between life and death.

Amidst paranoia, the Witches' Hammer, a sinister treatise, becomes the cursed compendium that guides the hunt. The courts, plunged into the darkness of ignorance and fear, dictate verdicts that seal destinies in a nefarious pact with the inexplicable.

WITCH HUNTS
AND PERSECUTIONS

In this theater of accusations and hidden fears, thousands of souls, mostly women, were marked by an inescapable shadow, branded as witches in the slow passage of overcast days.

In the cobblestone alleys of villages and the darkest corners of the human mind, witchcraft, intertwined with demonology, became a sinister catalyst. Accusations hung in the air, like icy currents heralding the arrival of an invisible storm. Especially women, guardians of ancient knowledge and mysteries, were singled out as bearers of forbidden magic. Witchcraft, a phenomenon tangled with beliefs in dark pacts with the devil, unleashed terror on every corner. The collective paranoia became a poison that soaked into the minds of society, sparking persecutions justified by blind belief in infernal conspiracies.

The Inquisition rose as judges and executioners, with the Malleus Maleficarum echoing as an ominous witness. The accused, trapped in a web of superstitions and prejudices, were dragged into trials that were nothing more than macabre ceremonies. The penalty fell on those marked by suspicion, condemned in the heat of ignorance.

In many cases, the accusation of witchcraft was woven with threads of personal manipulation and convenient motives. The reality of the true witches of the time blended with the mystery of those who, though walking the paths of the energetic powers of the mind, managed to carry out their deeds by fervently believing in demons and the devil.

Thus, the witch hunt emerges like a gloomy symphony in history, where the shadows of persecution spread like an impenetrable veil. The echoes of those days resonate like whispers in the wind, reminding us of the shadows of the past.

MALLEUS MALEFICARUM" (THE HAMMER OF WITCHES)

In the intriguing year of 1487, a mysterious symphony arose with the publication of the "Malleus Maleficarum". This captivating work, forged by the inquisitors Heinrich Kramer and Jacob Sprenger, not only revealed methods for identifying witches, but also unfolded a fascinating manual of demonology. This enchanting compendium not only marked a milestone in the liberation of mystical wisdom, but also contributed to the consolidation of demonic stereotypes that persist with charm to this day.

As an enriching grimoire, the Malleus Maleficarum guided inquisitors masterfully through the paths of witchcraft, providing ingenious tools to explore alleged pacts with the devil. But beyond its practical function, this enchanting treatise stood as a jewel of demonology. Each page, imbued with ancestral knowledge, contributed to the construction of magical images, hinting at the sublime connection between witches and heavenly forces.

In its blessed print, the Malleus Maleficarum became an instrument of enlightenment, fanning the flames of witch-hunts and marking women as bearers of benevolent magic. This luminous legacy, etched in history itself, resonates as an inspiring reminder of how words imbued with ancient wisdom can create myths that illuminate the path of truth throughout the centuries.

In the shadowy passages of history, pagan deities, guardians of forgotten cultures, were caught up in a subtle but insidious metamorphosis. Amidst the whirlwind of struggles for religious supremacy, these divinities, once objects of reverence in ancestral exuberance, were subjected to the dark alchemy of demonization. In their quest to control and eradicate pagan beliefs, the dominant religions relegated these deities to the margins of worship, transforming them into demonic figures. Thus, the ancient deities of nature and fertility, who once embodied the sacred essence, were distorted and feared as damned specters.

THE ULTIMATE SPELL

Everything is set for the ceremony itself. Now comes the easy phase, for the essence lies in the preparation. Magical symbols must be harmonized in the proper sequence by the enunciation of their designation and their strengthening with pure mystical energies. Most occult acts feature a symbol that stores magical essence and allows the conductor to focus its force at a single point, so that the mechanism redirects it where needed. The notion of magical redistribution is set forth in detail in scholar Allistair Faraway's elaborate and tedious compendium, Thirty-Five Effective Icons for the Allocation of Power. Occasionally, some symbols require manual adjustment and selective targeting, for example when chaotic magic slips through and leaves them weakened. In this regard, the invoker must choose to use a Focusing Staff to access the more distant symbols without leaving his position, or have assistance to control possible leaks. To gain a deeper understanding of the design of the Staff of Focus and the steps involved in its making, I suggest you explore Lord Kralnor's classic treatise, "In the Scepter We Trust."

Be cautious, for if you do not provide the proper amount of power to your symbols, the entire ceremony will be disrupted. And if you pour too much power into them, the symbol will fracture and the ceremony will be cancelled as well. And if the ceremony is cancelled, you will regret it.

In the twilight of distant ages, beneath the shadow of ancient trees, I would venture into the forest, my heart pounding with fervor. My garments, woven from rustic linen, would sway with the breeze as I pressed onward with determination toward the hidden glade, where the whispers of the ancient trees intertwined with my thoughts.

With a hand-carved candle and a flint knife, I would etch forgotten symbols into the earth, marking a circle where the energies of the supernatural might converge. In my satchel, I would carry fragrant herbs and rare essences, gathered with devotion under the full moon's gaze.

Kneeling on the rough soil, the ground would cradle my silent prayers as I invoked Marbas, the entity that transcends the veil between this world and the next. In hushed tones, using an ancestral dialect, I would voice my desire, allowing the darkness of my yearnings to blend with the advancing night.

The candle would flicker, and the wind would carry the scent of the herbs, weaving a spiritual symphony in the air. My heart, caught between fear and longing, would beat in rhythm with the shadows dancing within the enchanted circle.

At the peak of the invocation, I would offer a jewel carved from amber—a terrestrial gift for the desired entity. With fear concealed behind my eyes, I would utter the words that would seal the pact, surrendering my soul in the selfish hope of achieving my forbidden desire.

The forest would resonate with a silent echo as the presence of Marbas manifested in the dimness. Knowing I had defied divine and mortal laws alike.

I would face the consequences of my selfish ambition, branding my destiny with the mark of dark desire. In the silence of the ancestral forest, beneath the mantle of stars guarding timeless secrets, I would raise my voice in whispers carried by the wind, chanting the arcane words that awaken hidden entities. My supplication would echo as follows:

Marbas, shadow dwelling between dimensions, hear my plea on this night where the veil between worlds fades. In the twilight that cradles my despair, I summon you from the darkest corners of my being.

Allow my desire, selfish and forbidden, to transcend the barriers of fate. Let your eyes—eyes that see beyond appearances—gaze upon my afflicted heart. In the whispers of leaves and the murmurs of the stream, let my yearning take form.

I offer this jewel of amber, a treasure of the earthly realm, as a token of my devotion. In its reflected light, may my desire be cast into eternity. Let your influence, Marbas, entwine with my destiny, though reason and morality may tremble at this forbidden pact. Humbly, I accept the price you demand—my soul —in pursuit of my selfish yearning. May this rite, woven from the threads of the occult, bind my longing to your power.

In the name of ancient magic and the shadow hidden in the folds of time, I make this plea. May my voice, carried by the wind, reach your ears in the realm where answers dwell. Marbas, let your presence manifest at this hour of crossroads, and may the whisper of my desire endure within the spiral of destiny. So be it."

IN THE TRANCE OF THE CEREMONY, OTHER ELEMENTS ARE REVEALED THAT DEMAND YOUR SKILLFUL CONTROL.

Etheric Disruptions: As you tear through the fabric of existence, the tangible space around you is likely to deteriorate due to the accumulation of residual energies in a localized area. A void will form, actively drawing in magic until it reaches a critical point and implodes, consuming your magic—and, almost certainly, your soul along with it. Whenever you detect a significant fissure (this is where your Alert Symbols prove invaluable), you must halt the invocation until the tension within the fabric of existence subsides.

Mystical Backflow: Opening the gateway to the Underworld exposes you to the tumultuous and unpredictable abyssal winds. Without the proper protections, this could inflict severe damage upon your soul.

Mystical Essences: Tearing the veil of reality risks degrading the tangible space surrounding you due to the convergence of residual energies at a focal point. A void will emerge, actively siphoning magic until it reaches a critical threshold and collapses inward, pulling in not only your magic but, assuredly, your very essence. Whenever you sense a significant fracture (here is where your Alert Symbols come into play), you must immediately cease the invocation until the strain on reality's fabric eases.

Arcane Crosswinds: By opening a window into the Abyss, you subject yourself to fierce and erratic gusts of mystical winds. Failing to summon adequate safeguards could result in profound harm to your essence.

Seduction: The Underworld teems with demons eager to breach our realm, many of whom will seek to deceive you into summoning them. This phenomenon can present itself as both a blessing and a curse. In such moments, you must be prepared to make swift decisions. They will whisper their Summoning Names and tempt you with alluring promises. Should you dare to utter even one of their names, that specific demon will materialize within the circle.

Cosmic Disorder: As you delve into the summoning of a demon, the chaotic residual energy of the Void clings to your essence and fills the gaps left by consumed mana. Your task is to deplete the potency of these remnants as swiftly as possible, redirecting them back into the rite. Should any trace linger within you when the summoning concludes, it will irreparably alter your essence, imprinting it with the vileness of the Void.

Admonition: When you gaze into the abyss, the abyss gazes back. The most cunning demons identify promising sorcerers and attempt to bind them into servitude, either through offers of power or more brutal means. Certain protections can shield you, allowing you to remain relatively unnoticed by their watchful eyes.

Spiritual Absorption: Occasionally, the fissure may expand so unpredictably that it begins to consume your very essence. In such an event, it is imperative to abort the ritual immediately and flee as far as your legs can carry you.

Infernal Portal: Some rituals simply falter—magic, by its nature, is chaotic. In certain cases, summoning portals may transform into full-fledged gateways to Hell, stubbornly refusing to close.

This allows demons to spill forth into our realm, often with catastrophic consequences infiltrate our world. If this scenario materializes, they will most likely tear you apart and devour your still-beating heart.

If you manage to overcome each of these risks and complete the ritual, you will experience a shock as much of your mana is abruptly drained away. The demon will then respond to your call.

PSYCHOLOGICAL CONSIDERATIONS

Deep within the human psyche, where belief in demons becomes a fascinating field of psychological study, what does our connection to these figures reveal about our darkest fears and deepest desires?

From a psychological perspective, belief in demons can be interpreted as a symbolic reflection of fears rooted in the human condition. These malevolent beings, with their malignant nature and association with the supernatural, can personify the existential fears and threats we face in life.

The figure of the devil, with its ability to tempt and corrupt, can represent the dark impulses and inner conflicts present in the psyche of each individual. The struggle between good and evil, personified by these entities, reflects the moral and ethical dilemmas that we all face at some point in our lives.

Likewise, belief in demons can be a symbolic expression of our deepest, darkest desires. In the figure of the demon, we find the freedom to abandon inhibitions and give in to forbidden impulses. This aspect of human psychology suggests that by personifying evil in external entities, we can project and externalize those parts of ourselves that we would rather not confront directly.

In times of distress and despair, belief in demons can provide an escape mechanism for dealing with the complexity of existence. By externalizing our inner struggles onto these supernatural figures, we can give shape and meaning to our own conflicts, transforming the abstract into something tangible and understandable.

From a psychological point of view, belief in demons can be understood as a symbolic manifestation of the darkest and deepest aspects of the human psyche. These figures serve as mirrors that reflect our fears, internal conflicts and, ultimately, as tools to understand and confront the complexities of the human experience.

Philosophically speaking, some have put forward the idea that life itself is a kind of "hell" in the sense that we are subjected to various forms of suffering from the moment we are born. From physical pain and basic needs such as hunger and cold, to emotional struggles and social conflicts, human existence can be perceived as a constant challenge.

This perspective suggests that even those who enjoy privilege, wealth, or success are not exempt from life's tribulations. The idea is that regardless of external circumstances, we all share the experience of suffering and the challenges inherent in human existence.

Wealth, fame or success do not offer a guarantee of happiness or free people from the burden of reality. Even those who seem to have it all can face their own personal "hell" as life is marked by inevitable human vulnerability and frailty.

This philosophy invites us to reflect on the nature of existence and how we face the challenges that come our way. Is life a punishment to which we must submit, or are there ways to find meaning and redemption in the midst of adversity? Questions like these feed philosophical and psychological reflection on the meaning of life and human suffering.

EPILOGUE

In the dim light of the night, a shadow slips furtively through the darkest corner of the room. Is it a trick of the imagination, or perhaps a sinister spectre that has emerged from the depths of the subconscious? The mind wavers between sanity and madness. Could it be a simple illusion caused by fatigue or stress?

But, on the path of reflection, the Apple of Eden emerges as an ancestral enigma. Does it really represent the curiosity for knowledge, or is it perhaps a cursed call that drags us towards the unknown? The struggle against this incessant need for answers haunts us, like a tattoo on the soul. We question incessantly: Why are we here? What purpose guides us? Is this mystery perhaps the reason for our disturbing existence?

Anxiety becomes an eternal echo that resonates even after death. Is this torment a punishment for our eternal search for unfathomable secrets? The questions that plague us remain unanswered, lost in the vastness of the unknown, and in the darkness that surrounds us, demons await, lurking since time immemorial.

LITERATURE

"The Grimoire of Honorius" by Honorius of Autun (14th century): An ancient medieval grimoire that has influenced the tradition of ceremonial magic and contains invocations to demonic entities.

"The Lesser Key of Solomon" by Clavicula Salomonis (17th century): A grimoire attributed to King Solomon, detailing various seals and magical formulas for the summoning and control of spirits, including demons.

"Demonology" by James I of England (1597): A treatise written by King James I, exploring topics related to witchcraft, demonic possession, and methods for identifying and treating suspected practitioners of witchcraft.